ORDINANCE OF FREEDOM

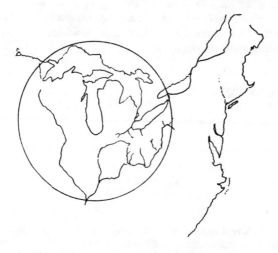

Robert V. Van Trees

Author and Publisher

ISBN 0-9616282-1-9

Library of Congress 86-50013

Published by Robert V. Van Trees
P. O. Box 2062
Fairborn, OH   45324-8062

Manufactured by Apollo Books, 107 Lafayette St., Winona, MN   55987

PRINTED IN THE UNITED STATES OF AMERICA

To the Fort Recovery Historical Society, for their enterprise and fortitude in preserving the memory of those who made the supreme sacrifice on the banks of the Wabash, this book is respectfully dedicated.

AUTHOR'S NOTE

No one can write a "primer" of this kind out of his head and the author is indebted to not only those whose personalized accounts make it possible to catch a glimpse of our nation's critical "diaper years," but the countless librarians from the banks of the Susquehannah in Harrisburg, Pennsylvania to the shores of Lake Mendota in Madison, Wisconsin, whose efforts aided in locating such documents. A major problem in researching any topic dealing with the fascinating history of the "United States Territory Northwest of the River Ohio" is knowing where to end, not where to begin—the information available in our country's archives is varied and extensive. This narration then, is the product of many minds whose donations to posterity were examined in an effort to provide a brief summary of events leading to the promulgation of the Ordinance of 1787 and implementation of its provisions under the controversial leadership of Governor Arthur St. Clair—a man who led hundreds to their death on the banks of the Wabash in early November of 1791.

The Great Seal on the cover was sketched many years ago by the author during a visit to the Main Library of Ohio State University in Columbus, Ohio. Designed in relief and framed with wreaths, the Seals of the United States, Northwest Territory, State of Ohio, and Ohio State University are indelibly carved in stone above the entrance of the William Oxley Thompson Library, which was dedicated in January of 1913. Among the treasured literary possessions of the author's grandfather, a voracious reader, was a time-worn copy of the *Ohio State Lantern* dated January 8, 1913. This student weekly publication indicated the Northwest Territory Seal is of obscure origin, was first used by Governor St. Clair in 1788, and the latin inscription means, "He has planted a better than the former!"

Entrance, William Oxley Thompson Library
Columbus, Ohio

TABLE OF CONTENTS

PROLOGUE

Closely interwoven in the educational, cultural and business pursuits of the American is an awareness of the Constitution of the United States of America—insight into its provisions vary with each person's undertakings as some learn only the Preamble while others engage in activities prompting them to take advantage of the Fifth Amendment. Few people in our twentieth century society have not heard of the guaranties of the First Amendment or the repeal of the Eighteenth Amendment which invoked prohibition in a country which refused to stay "dry."

But, promulgated in the same time frame 200 years ago—and a charter equally as important to the cherished principles and future of this nation—was a masterful statute enacted in New York City during the summer of 1787 while delegates from all states except Rhode Island were toiling over drafting the Constitution in Philadelphia. Although most Americans become aware in school of the "Ordinance of 1787"—or the "Ordinance of Freedom" as it is called in some historical accounts—rare is the person who is knowledgeable of the far-reaching provisions of the historic charter which became the organic law of the vast area once known only as the Territory of the United States Northwest of the River Ohio. Providing for free schools, free churches, free soil, free men, and establishment of government in the region northwest of the Ohio River, the principles enunciated in the Ordinance of 1787 are deeply ingrained in our heritage.

Washed by the waters of the Great Lakes on the north, the Ohio River on the south, the Mississippi on the west, and watered by the many streams flowing through the fertile fields of the region, the virgin wilderness country was hailed by its immigrants as "the promised land." In this vast area the varied interests and divergent cultures of the pioneer settlers from the thirteen discordant and contentious states met—it was "America's first melting pot" according to one 19th century historian. In this first colony of the fledgling nation was born a colonial policy unique in the world—one of America's great contributions to government which has been a source of guidance to learned men and women who have read this Ordinance of Freedom. Through this "common child" of the new republic a formula of eminence among all the governments of mankind was established.

With the freedom-loving and land-hungry settlers' surge westward, this historic Magna Carta of the Northwest Territory gave recognition by the new government of those most cherished principles of our fundamental law—the rights of men. Like the Magna Carta—the cornerstone of English liberty which King John of England reluctantly agreed to in the meadow of Runnymead June 1, 1215—the Ordinance of Freedom guaranteed certain civil and political liberties to the residents of the Northwest Territory, among these being the right to life, liberty, and the pursuit of happiness. It was the 32nd President of the United States, Franklin Delano Roosevelt, who said of this historic charter:

"The principles therein embodied served as a highway, broad and safe, over which poured the westward march of our civilization. On this plan was the United States built."

CHAPTER 1

The Westward Tide

"The extensive and fertile regions of the West will yield
a most happy asylum to those who, fond of domestic
enjoyment, are seeking personal independence."

General George Washington

Eight years after the embattled farmers drove the British from the
bridge at Concord, General Washington declared the Revolutionary
War at an end on April 10, 1783 and the treaty of peace was signed
five months later on September 3rd at the Hotel d'York on the rue
Jacob in Paris—Benjamin Franklin, John Adams, John Jay, and
Henry Lamens signed for the United States and Commissioner David
Hartley represented Great Britian. The Treaty of Paris was ratified by
the United States May 12, 1784.

Thus the eight years of war and two decades of bitter agitation
ended and the creative energies of the American people were freed.
The cost of the Revolutionary War has been estimated at slightly in
excess of one hundred million dollars—two hundred years later the
cost of a single B-1 bomber is estimated in excess of that figure and
the Department of Defense talks of a proposed military budget of
264.4 billion dollars. In the exacting science of government
budgeting the decimal point imparts a note of grotesque precision to a
quantity beyond imagination.

The Revolutionary War was fought largely by patriotic idealists
with, and in sympathy of, the so-called common people. It was
financed reluctantly by the more prosperous class and, despite the

1

zeal of their efforts and support of the common causes, there were some patriots who feared the new government would be sorely pressed to function without the financial support of Great Britain.

With the end of the war, representatives of the brave new republic were now faced with an awesome responsibility—the government of a populace who yearned for the "freedoms" of the new land. Now it was more than just those who were looking for the elusive northwest passage to China as in the pre-war years— or the fur traders and missionaries who had ventured far into the wilderness northwest of the Ohio River. From the 17th century onward French fur traders and dedicated religious teachers had extended their activities among the Indians and encouraged resistance to the colonial interest of the British who watched the French activities with a suspicious eye.

In 1497 John and Sebastian Cabot, father and son, had crossed the Atlantic and landed in Nova Scotia. The following year they again sailed the Atlantic and traveled as far south as North Carolina giving England its claim to the mainland of North America by right of discovery. In 1607, one year before Samuel Champlain established his colony at Quebec, the Jamestown Colony of Virginia became the first permanent English settlement in America. Queen Elizabeth I of England, the "Virgin Queen," granted the territory of Virginia to Sir Walter Raleigh in 1584 and he dutifully named the region in her honor. Connecticut's charter was signed by King Charles II in 1662. The charters and patents granted by the English sovereigns in those early years indicated the land grant extended "from ocean to ocean."

As early as 1534 Jacques Cartier sailed the Atlantic from France and traveled up the St. Lawrence River. Champlain ascended the St. Lawrence in 1608 and sailed across the Great Lakes—he was appointed Governor of Canada by King Louis XIII of France in 1620. Frenchmen Radisson and Groseilliers were in the Minnesota region and came in contact with the Sioux Indians in 1659. At the eastern end of Lake Superior as early as 1668 French missionary and explorer Father Jacques Marquette founded a settlement at Sault Sainte Marie. The influence of the French-Catholic missionaries upon

2

the Indians and white settlers of the Great Lakes region was far reaching.

Probably the first white man to explore the Wisconsin area, and while seeking a route to Cathay, China, Jean Nicolet (1598-1652) is believed to have landed in 1634 on the shores of Green Bay where he met the Winnebago Indians. Prairie du Chien and Green Bay were early settlements of the region called "Quisconsin." Intrigued by the potential of the area's rich fur trade, in 1673 Louis Joliet and Father Marquette traversed this same region and paddled down the Mississippi. It was Perrot who laid claim to the upper Mississippi country for France in 1689— it was this same Frenchman who discovered lead mines in the late 1600s around the present Galena, Illinois where Negro slaves were used in the mines until 1820.

In the early 1700s Cahokia and Kaskaskia were busy French trading posts close to the Mississippi River—links in a chain of proposed forts from the St. Lawrence to the Gulf of Mexico. In 1712 the Illinois River was the northern border of the Louisiana Territory. Captain Pierre Joseph Celeron de Bienville's expedition in 1749 down the Ohio River, up the Great Miami River, and through the wilderness to the Maumee River, was looked upon by Great Britain as ominous. The English countered with Christopher Gist's expedition in 1750 and, in accordance with George Washington's suggestion following his 1753 visit to the western Pennsylvania area, Governor Robert Dinwiddie of Virginia sent troops in 1754 to build a fort at the strategic junction of the Allegheny and Monongahela Rivers where Pittsburgh now stands. The French and Indians forced the militia to abandon the post and built Fort Duquesne on the site but it was taken from them by English troops under General Forbes in 1758 and Fort Pitt was erected.

The French and English interests were bound to clash and came to a head in the French and Indian War which started in 1754. By a treaty signed in Paris on February 18, 1763 the war ended and all land northwest of the Ohio River and east of the Mississippi was ceded to England. Now it was the British who had to contend with the fever of the westward movement.

France's dream of an empire in the New World actually came to an end with the Battle of Quebec in 1759 when General James Wolfe led his men up the steep cliffs to the Plains of Abraham against General Marquis de Montcalm. Both of these leaders died in that battle and General George Townsend took Wolfe's place in the victory celebration by the British troops. It was a relatively unknown lieutenant from Scotland who, under General Wolfe, scaled the heights of Abraham and helped wrest Quebec and Canada from France for Great Britian. The lieutenant, Arthur St. Clair, was later to pledge his allegiance to the colonies of his adopted country and become the first governor of the Northwest Territory.

Colonies were regarded as dependencies to be governed by the mother country for the promotion of its own advantage. Great Britain wanted no quarrel with the Indians and in an effort to thwart the "westward tide" King George III announced his Royal Proclamation Line of 1763 forbidding the settlers moving west of the Allegheny Mountains—he failed to reckon with the driving spirit of the rugged pioneers who pushed relentlessly westward despite the rigor and danger beyond the demarcating mountains.

Chief Pontiac of the Ottawa nation had kept the French hopes in the northwest alive until 1765 when France's fleur-de-lis was lowered at Fort de Chatres along the Mississippi and English dominion was effected. By the Quebec Act of 1774 Great Britain annexed the Illinois area to the Province of Quebec and proclaimed the frontiers of New York and Pennsylvania provinces extended as far west as the Mississippi. In giving away land previously granted, the king ignored the colony's charters which included "land from ocean to ocean" and this stimulated a rebellious spirit among the colonists. Such intolerable acts also caused settlers in the area of what is now Illinois to sympathize with the American colonists during the Revolutionary War and they greeted with open arms the arrival of George Rogers Clark and his "Long Knives" in 1778. Even before the Revolutionary War the British Ministry decided to maintain a standing army in America and tax the colonies to support it—the colonies balked and this marked the death of the old British Empire.

The region along the Ohio River which is now Indiana had been traversed by Robert Cavalier De La Salle (1643-1687) in 1670 and in the early 1700s French traders were at the site where Fort Wayne

4

now stands. In 1722 the French built Fort Quiatenon southwest of the present Lafayette, Indiana. In the early 1700s a French fur-trading village along the Wabash river was one of the oldest settlements in that region and in 1732 a fort was established there under the command of the Sieur de Vincennes— his name was given to the town when he was killed by the Indians in 1736. The fortification at Vincennes became Fort Sackville and George Rogers Clark captured it early in 1779 during an expedition authorized by Governor Patrick Henry of Virginia.

Closer to east coast settlements, but still deep in the wilderness territory, as early as 1761 Moravian missionary Frederick Post from Pennsylvania built along the Tuscarawas River what some historians say was the first "American's house" in the region now known as Ohio. In the same area a decade later, on May 3, 1772, two more Moravian missionaries—David Zeisberger and John Heckewelder—and some Christian Delawares began building Indian villages at Schoenbrunn, Lichtenau, and the ill-fated Gnadenhutten which was ravaged by white ruffians in March of 1782.

Farther to the south, and in ever increasing numbers, squatters "trespassed" in the region northwest of the Ohio River. Wiseman's Bottom, four miles above the mouth of the Muskinghum, was named after the man who made a clearing as entry right to 400 acres while Virginia still claimed the land. In a somewhat futile effort for recognition, the squatters elected William Hogland as governor of the territory north of the Ohio where they had taken up residence sans land title. It was of course illegal but in the year (1785) Fort Harmar was built—discouraging further encroachment by the squatters—Ensign John Armstrong reported:

"There are at the falls of the Hawkin (Hocking River) upwards of three hundred families and at the Muskinghum a number equal."

As Great Britain struggled with their frustrating efforts to halt the "westward tide" in the years before the Declaration of Independence was proclaimed, representatives of the independent-prone colonies had one thing in common—an increasing distrust of the mother country. The flames of rebellion were fanned by such things as the Stamp Act of 1765 and tax placed by the British Parliament on tea coming into the colonies which sparked the Boston Tea Party on December 16, 1773.

As early as 1754 there had been a convention in Albany and a call for a united effort against the Indians but the king would not tolerate such a union. Irked by the restraint on individual freedom, many of the colonists had struck out for the wilderness to the west presaging the advice of American journalist and politician Horace Greeley (1811-1872) who will be remembered as saying:

"Go West young man, go West!"

CHAPTER 2

The Declaration of Independence

"That these colonies are, and of right ought to be, free
and independent States; and that all political connections
between them and the State of Great Britain, is, and ought to
be, totally dissolved."

Resolution by Congress, July 2, 1776

Although there had been abortive efforts toward unity before, the
resolution introduced by Richard Henry Lee June 7, 1776 set in
motion a series of actions that led to its passage on July 2nd and the
subsequent Declaration of Independence two days later.

After Lexington and Concord, Congress asked Thomas
Jefferson to draft a "Declaration Of Causes And The Necessity Of
Taking Up Arms." The zeal of the patriot's words were too strong
and John Dickinson wrote a substitute resolution more moderate but
employing most of Jefferson's words. It was a resolution long in
coming and preceded by many years of growing unrest and
dissatisfaction with the mother country's intolerable acts.

Delegates of the First Continental Congress had gathered for the
first time at Carpenter's Hall in Philadelphia September 5, 1774. The
meeting had been called by the Massachusetts Assembly at the urging
of Harvard graduate Samuel Adams (1722-1803), a political leader
who stirred up discontent among the colonists in his public speeches.

He opposed the Stamp Act of 1765 and was a leader of the Friday night Boston Tea Party in December of 1773.

Danger to all of the colonies was seen in the acts of the British Parliament aimed against Massachusetts, especially the Boston Port Bill. Fifty-five delegates representing twelve colonies attended the initial meeting in Philadelphia including such personages as George Washington, Patrick Henry, Richard Henry Lee, Samuel Adams, John Adams, John Jay, Joseph Galloway, John Dickinson, and Peyton Randolph of Virginia who was chosen President of the First Continental Congress. Georgia sent no representative but agreed to support any plans made at the conference where equal voting power was given each colony.

The First Continental Congress was more interested in just treatment from Great Britain than in independence and a Declaration of Rights was adopted October 14, 1774 setting forth the delegate's position concerning taxation and trade by the colonies. Each independent-prone colony held strongly to its belief of the right to draw up its laws on all subjects except foreign trade. Probably the boldest act of the inexperienced Congress was to set up the American Association which bound the colonists to not trade with Great Britain or use British goods until the mother country's trade and taxation policies had been changed. Plans were made to hold another Congress in May of 1775 as the delegates prepared to disband.

But colonial policy did not change and the colonies drew close to war with the fighting between Massachusetts farmers and British troops under General Thomas Gage in the spring of 1775. On the night of April 18, 1775 Paul Revere preceded British troops warning Samuel Adams and John Hancock of their intended arrest and telling the people to take arms—his historic ride on "Scheherazade" inspired Henry W. Longfellow to write "Paul Revere's Ride" in 1863.

Major John Pitcairn's British troops marched through Lexington the morning of April 19th to the accompaniment of sporadic gunfire and warning church bells and met the fury of the New England citizen troops just beyond Concord. The British retreated to Boston with heavy losses. It is reported that General Gage was livid as he observed his British troops being chased by the colonial patriots who were accompanied by a small band who repeatedly played the popular song, "Yankee Doodle."

Smoke from the engagement "by the rude bridge that arched the flood" had hardly cleared when the Second Continental Congress convened in Philadelphia May 10, 1775—now Benjamin Franklin, Thomas Jefferson, and John Hancock took part as Congress faced the duties of a government uniting the colonies for a war effort. An army was organized and, in accordance with the recommendation of John Adams, the stern disciplinarian George Washington was appointed "Commander in chief of all troops raised for the defense of American liberty."

On July 8, 1775 Congress issued a declaration setting forth the need to take up arms and the reasons for doing so. Two days later a final, and useless appeal, was made to King George III in an effort to right matters without war. But war was inevitable and with its outbreak the Second Continental Congress encouraged the colonies to set themselves up as states and appoint diplomatic agents to represent their individual interests in foreign countries.

The breach with Great Britain widened and on June 7, 1776 Richard Henry Lee introduced his resolution and it was passed by the Congress less than a month later. The resolution declared all political connection between the colonies and Great Britain ought to be totally dissolved and a committee composed of Benjamin Franklin, John Adams, Robert R. Livingston, and Thomas Jefferson was appointed to draw up a Declaration of Independence. Jefferson accepted the suggestion he frame such a document. With moving eloquence the Declaration Jefferson proposed set forth the basic philosophy of democracy and constitutionalism and with but a few changes the document was submitted to Congress on July 4, 1776 by Richard H. Lee of Virginia. It was quickly seconded by John Adams of Massachusetts, a statesman of high courage who was destined to be the second president of the United States.

The Declaration of Independence set forth in fervid terms the general principles of the rights of man and prompted a stormy debate wherein John Adams, the "Atlas of American Independence," defended the document with typical enthusiasm and fervor. Led by John Hancock, the first to sign this famous document with a sprawling signature which probably reflected the emotion of the moment, on August 2, 1776 fifty-five members of that august body of delegates signed the historic proclamation.

The general public did not learn the actual words of the stirring Declaration of Independence until July 8th. The ideas reflected in this historic document were not particularly new— the English themselves had used many of the same aims to justify their "Glorious Revolution" in 1688 when they deposed King James II and Parliament passed a Bill of Rights the following year—one of the three legal guarantees of English liberty. The simplicity of the wording stirred the hearts of everyone in the colonies. When the British raided Washington during the War of 1812, this famous document was secreted in Leesburg, Virginia. Rare is a person who does not recognize the inspiring words of the Declaration of Independence of the thirteen united states as reads:

"We hold these truths to be self-evident, that all men are created equal, that they are endowed by their Creator with certain inalienable Rights, that among these are Life, Liberty, and the pursuit of Happiness."

Four score and seven years after the Declaration of Independence was adopted by Congress, the President of the United States reminded the nation it was "conceived in liberty and dedicated to the proposition that all men are created equal." Those were the moving words said by Abraham Lincoln at Gettysburg a few months after the battle which marked the turning point of the war between the states. In July of 1863 the Confederate army under General Robert E. Lee met the Union army commanded by General George C. Meade and after a three day battle, Lee's army retreated. Later that same year President Lincoln, in a brief and simple speech, concluded saying:

"That this Nation under God shall have a new birth of freedom and that government of the people, by the people, for the people, shall not perish from this earth."

President Lincoln's address contains only two hundred sixty-seven words but those words proclaimed November 19, 1863 still stir the deepest feelings of the nation's people.

CHAPTER 3

Articles of Confederation

"There is a tide in the affairs of men, which, taken at the
flood, leads on to fortune."

William Shakespeare

Having proclaimed their independence, the delegates from the
colonies now set about drawing up an outline for a permanent central
government and union of states which resulted in the unwieldy and
undefendable Articles of Confederation—it was the epitome of
forced cooperation for mutual defense. To declare themselves free
and independent was one thing for them to do but to compel Great
Britain to acknowledge it and give up her claims was quite a different
matter and the colonies realized they must work together to
accomplish this. On September 9, 1776 the country's lawmakers
decided on "United States" instead of the proposed "United
Colonies." It was a start!

Leadership of the Continental Congress changed several times.
In addition to Peyton Randolph who served twice, presidents of the
Continental Congress were Henry Middleton, John Hancock, Henry
Laurens, John Jay, Samuel Huntington, Thomas McKean, John
Hanson, Elias Boudinot, Thomas Mifflin, Richard Henry Lee,
Nathan Gorham, Arthur St. Clair, and Cyrus Griffin.

The rush of war caused the proposed Articles of Confederation
to be laid aside when the first draft was written but they were finally
completed November 15, 1777 and submitted to the respective states

for approval. Most gave their quick approval but there was the question of the vast territory northwest of the Ohio River.

A major stumbling block of the Congress in uniting the thirteen colonies in a permanent government was the strong feeling of "state's rights." The feeling was so strong that even the weak national organization provided by the Articles of Confederation was not adopted without many objections. Many of the large states had colonial claims to land lying west of the Appalachian Mountains and the statesmen of six coastal states insisted the territory west of Pennsylvania and north of the Ohio River belonged not to America but to the original colonies under charter from King Charles II who had written "from coast to coast" in their patents. Connecticut had received her charter as early as April 20, 1662.

Fearing they might be swallowed up, the small states demanded certain western lands be ceded to the central government. Maryland in particular demanded all share in the wealth won by "common blood and treasure." Out of long debate evolved a new political concept for the government of the former dependencies of Great Britain and states having claims to western lands were to cede them to the central government to be administered for the benefit of all. Congress in turn pledged these lands would be organized into states and admitted to the Union on a basis of equality with existing states. Adamant in her convictions, Maryland was the last to ratify the Articles of Confederation and did not do so until March 1, 1781—only six months before the fall of Yorktown and not before she had reason to believe the colonies would cede their western lands to control of Congress.

Meanwhile the Second Continental Congress operated under great difficulties because it was a group without legal authority except when it acted with the unanimous consent of the represented states. The Second Congress continued to work with less and less power until March 1, 1781 when a new Congress, authorized by the Articles of Confederation, took over its tasks. But, although the government of the Confederation came into being in 1781, it was first given concrete application in the Ordinance of 1787. Thus, a major step in the establishment of a real nationality depended to a great extent upon the Northwest Territory and was a major factor in

13

determining the beginning of our nation as the United States of America.

Between 1781 and 1786 New York in 1781, Virginia in 1784, Massachusetts in 1785, and finally Connecticut in 1786 gave up their charter claims in face of Maryland's stubborn insistence it would not approve the Articles of Confederation until they agreed to do so. But Virginia and Connecticut in ceding their claims reserved for a future use a portion of her charter lands. Connecticut reserved 3,500,000 acres extending 120 miles east from the Pennsylvania border bounded on the south by the 41st parallel and on the west by a line which is now the western boundary of Huron and Erie counties in Ohio. This "Western Reserve" was later disposed of in two separate actions, with 500,000 acres (Firelands) being divided in 1792 among the victims of fires set by the British during the Revolutionary War and the remainder sold in 1795 with Moses Cleaveland acting as general agent for the purchaser—an area which was called New Connecticut. In May of 1800 the Connecticut Assembly passed an act renouncing all her claims to land in the Northwest Territory.

In negotiating the terms of the Treaty of Paris in 1782, John Adams—who had been appointed by Congress September 27, 1779 to negotiate peace terms with the British—wisely insisted the western boundary of the Northwest Territory be the Mississippi River and not the Ohio River as Great Britain wanted. With a favorable treaty of peace concluded wherein Great Britain ceded the land west of Pennsylvania and north of the Ohio River to the United States which she had received from France in 1763, the fledgling government now took up the problems of an area which included the land presently in Ohio, Indiana, Illinois, Michigan, Wisconsin, and that portion of Minnesota east of the Mississippi River.

Having won its independence, the new republic faced an assortment of conflicting interests of the states plus the many faceted issues of the westward movement. And despite the provisions of the Treaty of Paris concluded in 1783, Great Britain and the Indians were in actual possession of most of the land north and west of the Ohio River—a possession they did not surrender until much later. Thus, the British had to be expelled and the Indians "removed, absorbed, or extirpated" as one public official declared pedantically.

14

With a disbanded army after 1783 and no money in the treasury, any talk of military action in the Northwest Territory seemed just that ... talk!

The delegates who sat down together after the war to discuss use of the western land won "by common blood and treasure" represented varying interests from the easy-going folks of the south who chose agrarian pursuits to the energetic New Englanders who leaned toward manufacture and trade. The Puritans of New England, radical in their beliefs and zealous in their teachings, had little in common with the settlers of Virginia, Georgia, and the Carolinas. Even in New England, Connecticut and Rhode Island had been split off the Massachusetts colony because of religious disputes. Sandwiched between the incongruous groups of the north and south were the Dutch of New York, the Swedes of Delaware, the Catholics of Maryland, and the Quakers and Germans of Pennsylvania. With such diverse religions, nationalities, and economic and moral distinctions—and their respective charters—it is amazing they were able to get along together at all.

Although the Articles of Confederation provided a semblance of unification, a major weakness of "the system" was that Congress could not raise money by taxation to pay the government's obligations. The only way to get money was for Congress to ask for it and this proved both difficult and sometimes fruitless—seventy-five percent of the funds requested were not received and even the government's obligations to the army could not be liquidated. Repeated attempts to amend the Articles of Confederation failed because every state had to agree on any amendment. Absence of a strong executive head and a national court were contributing weaknesses and the thirteen states began drifting apart.

CHAPTER 4

The Newburgh Petition

"If I were a young man, just preparing to begin the world, or if in advanced life and had a family to provide for, I know of no region where I would rather fix my habitation than in some part of this region."

General George Washington

In an effort to encourage enlistments in 1776 Congress had pledged grants of land for military service. Virginia had given such bounties for service in earlier wars against the French and Indians and it seemed an appropriate way to stimulate interest in enlistments. But, at the time the plan was formulated, the government really owned no public lands for such use.

Now, with the Revolutionary War over, the government still owned no land and the treasury was empty. To make matters even more awkward, Congress had no authority to raise revenues and could only recommend to the several states more liberal grants of money and supplies for the army which in 1783 had not been disbanded. With the official end of the war there were many who were still unpaid for their services and some returned to their homes penniless while others waited for their earned compensation.

Envisioning Congress should purchase land from the Indians to fulfill the bounty promises, in June of 1783 Bridgadier General Rufus Putnam initiated, and Colonel Timothy Pickering at Camp Newburgh put in written form, "Propositions For Settling A New State By Such Officers And Soldiers Of The Federal Army As Shall

Associate For That Purpose." This plan has alternately been called the "Newburgh Petition," the "Pickering Plan," and the "Army Plan" but it was the crystalized expression from men who had fought to establish a new nation and was signed by men of the Continental Line as fundamental to their hopes, ambitions, and plans. The provisions of this document which was submitted to the Congress in June of 1783 prayed the lawmakers would fulfill the pledge the government made in 1776 by assigning to the petitioners certain tracts of land which lay between the Ohio River and Lake Erie west of Pennsylvania. The Newburgh Petition bore a striking resemblance to the Ordinance of 1787 which would be enacted four years later.

The humble, and relatively little known Newburgh Petition, was more than just a request for land—it set forth certain provisions of government as essential to the petition. Unfortunately, some of the land identified in the petition was still claimed by states under charter granted by the King of England. In addition, the Newburgh Petition contained the then radical prohibition of slavery proviso.

Among the more than 280 signers of the petition, and one of its most influential advocates, was General Putnam who planned— if Congress approved the plan—to form a colony and move to the Ohio River valley. Putnam strongly believed a friendship with the Indians would secure traffic through them and provide a measure of frontier security. He was of the further opinion approval of the petition would promote land sales in the new territory and help the government treasury as well as preclude the possibility of returning the northwest region to any European power.

Putnam remembered General Washington's oft repeated expressions of faith in the future of the western territory and in his letter of June 16, 1783 to his former commanding officer he requested support for the Newburgh Petition. Putnam also suggested the territory be surveyed into six mile townships and a portion of the land be set apart for the support of the maintenance of free schools and the ministry. Although Washington was unable to get Congress to take favorable action on the petition at that time, the plan undoubtedly led to the development of the principles evoked in the Ordinance of 1787.

George Washington, the man who was to become the first President of the United States in 1789, had more than a casual interest in the plan for and success of the first western colony. He remembered well the campfire talks at Logstown in 1753 wherein St. Pierre represented France and Washington spoke on behalf of Virginia's interests and suggested the French refrain from trespassing on English soil. It was at this conference where the Beaver empties into the Ohio River in western Pennsylvania that Chief Half King of the Six Nations ordered both to "move off" the Indian lands. The Indian's order fell on deaf ears and in the French and Indian War of 1754-1763 England emerged victorious and France ceded the territory northwest of the Ohio River in a treaty signed in Paris in 1763.

But that was more than two decades ago and in the interim Washington had selected some 40,000 acres of land in the Virginia and Ohio country and—along with William Crawford—had visited the region at the mouth of the Great Kanawha River in 1770 where the future President laid claim to 10,000 acres. In counsel with members of his command during the Revolutionary War the general often urged they consider the merits of settlement in the Ohio valley. In response to Putnam's repeated request for assistance in April of 1784, Washington used his influence to get Congress to direct the paymaster general to adjust the accounts of the Revolutionary War veterans and issue Continental Certificates of the sum which might appear on such settlements as the Superintendent of Finance might direct. Unfortunately, the United States Treasury was in a state of depletion and the certificates were worth less than one-sixth of their face value. The interest bearing certificates were known as "final settlements" but their depreciated value of twelve to sixteen cents on the dollar soon gave rise to the expression, "not worth a Continental."

But, worthless as they might appear to be, they could buy western land from the government provided the Indian "titles" to the land concerned could be quieted. When economic necessity prompted some veterans to consider selling land bounty warrants for paltry sums, it was George Washington who counseled the western lands would rise in value to twenty to fifty dollars an acre "as soon as the

Indians were cleared from the land" and he prophesized each land warrant would be worth a fortune.

In the darkest hour of the Revolutionary War a soldier is said to have asked General Washington:

"Sir, if the British drive us from the Atlantic seaboard, what will become of us?"

The General is reported to have replied without hesitation:

"Then we will retire to the valley of the Ohio and there we will be free!"

Thus, in both word and deed did Washington repeatedly reflect his support of the future of the Northwest Territory and he envisioned the veterans of the Revolutionary War would be a strong force in the development of that region. Washington also knew the people who had the ambition and ability to settle that territory were the type least likely to accept a government they did not like. The promulgators of the Ordinance of 1787 knew they could count on Washington for his support.

George Washington's time on earth ended with the 17th century and he died on the night of December 14, 1799. It was "Light Horse Harry" Lee of Washington's military staff during the Revolutionary War who voiced a perfect tribute to his leader saying:

"First in war, first in peace, first in the hearts of his countrymen!"

The final words Washington had written in his diary the day of his death were:

"Tis well."

CHAPTER 5

The Critical Years

"I have sworn on the altar of God eternal hostility against every form of tyranny over the mind of man."

Thomas Jefferson,
3rd President of the United States

A basic cornerstone of our civilization is the institution of private property and in the Ordinances of 1784 and 1785 provisions were enunciated for the survey and sale of land and set the pattern for the making of new states. But, despite the wisdom and intent of the drafters of these two statutes, they did not stimulate the positive action which followed the Ordinance of 1787.

In early March of 1784 a committee, chaired by Thomas Jefferson of Virginia, was appointed by Congress to formulate a temporary plan for government of the territory northwest of the Ohio River. The plan submitted by the committee on April 19th, and adopted four days later, proposed to divide the western territory by lines of latitude two degrees apart intersected by longitudinal lines drawn through the mouth of the Kanawha River and the Falls of Ohio (Louisville).

Jefferson envisioned a row of "buffer" states between the settled states of the East and those large and presumably more powerful states along the Mississippi River. As influential chairman of the committee, Jefferson's draft plan proposed to divide the territory into ten states with such names as Sylvania, Michigania, Assenisipia, Illinoia, Saratoga, Polypotamia, Chersonesus, Metropotamia,

Pelisipia, and Washington. The Congress accepted the system of territorial division but rejected the proposed names deciding to allow each area to choose its own name when it should enter the Union.

The plan submitted by Jefferson's committee was amended and approved April 23, 1784 and this Ordinance of 1784 lasted—on paper at least—until July 13, 1787 when the Congress of the Confederation adopted the Ordinance of 1787 which was specific in its provisions regarding the number of states to be formed from the Northwest Territory and included guidelines regarding boundaries which provoked controversy in future years with some states declaring the Ordinance of 1787 itself was unconstitutional.

Although the work accomplished by Thomas Jefferson and his committee in the Spring of 1784 may have contributed to the provisions of the Ordinance of 1784, historians note Jefferson was dispatched May 10, 1784 to Paris to assist Benjamin Franklin and John Adams in negotiation of treaties of commerce and his subsequent appointment as United States Minister to France necessitated his absence from this country until December of 1789 when he returned after having been appointed Secretary of State by President Washington. Jefferson's influence on the Ordinance of 1787 is questionable since the Ordinance promulgated by his committee contained none of the broad provisions found in the Ordinance of 1787 concerning religious freedom, the fostering of education, distribution of estates of intestates, the privilege of the writ of habeas corpus, trial by jury, moderation in fines and punishments, the taking of private property for public use (eminent domain), and interference of law with the obligation of private contracts. Under the Ordinance of 1784 no provision was made for the distribution or sale of land and under this statute no settlements were made in the northwest country. In addition, it did not contain the anti-slavery proviso and certainly not the articles of compact agreed upon three years later.

Judiciously reserving the Virginia Military District, in 1784 Virginia ceded to the central government her charter claims to the land north of the Ohio River but the Indian claims still stood in the way to prevent disposition of the lands by Congress. Some of these obstructions were removed by the Treaty of Fort McIntosh concluded

21

January 21, 1785 at the mouth of the Big Beaver River on the Ohio whereby—with certain reservations—the attending Delaware, Chippewa, Ottawa, the Wyandot sachems relinquished title to a large extent of land in the region now known as Ohio. But, as proved troublesome in the ensuing years, chiefs of the Shawnee and Miami villages were not signators to this treaty and they lived in the region ceded to the United States government.

In 1785 Congress commissioned Generals George Clark, Richard Butler, and Samuel Parsons to negotiate a treaty of peace with the Indians establishing boundaries which would insure everlasting friendship. General Butler dispatched Captain Finney from Fort Pitt down the Ohio River to the mouth of the Great Miami where he arrived on October 22nd and built a fortification close to the river which he called "Fort Finney." Here during January of 1786 such Indian personages as Tarhe the Crane, White Eyes, Captain Johnny, and Half King reluctantly "negotiated" on behalf of the Delawares, Ottawas, Wyandots, and Shawnees surrendering more of the land north and west of the Ohio River to the United States government. Blue Jacket, the youthful white-man-turned-Shawnee, viewed the campfire "negotiations" with great distrust of the white man whose way of life Marmaduke Van Swearingen had deserted in 1771.

On the 31st of January at Fort Finney Generals Butler, Clark, Ebenezer Zane, and Ephraim Lewis joined with the gathered red sachems to sign the treaty despite the obvious resentment which permeated the ceremony. Indicative of the bitterness of some of the Indians was Blue Jacket's action as he marched with 500 warriors against Fort Finney only two months later on April 6th. But nature intervened and a spring flood wiped out the fort along the Ohio River that Sunday morning only hours before the war party arrived. Along with Captain David Zeigler, Captain Finney marched his troops down the Ohio to a point opposite Louisville and erected another fort with the same name—but this time it was erected on high ground. The unfortunate early April flood probably saved the lives of the first fort's occupants.

By the Land Ordinance of 1785 enacted by Congress on May 20th, the government adopted a national system of surveys which was suggested by Rufus Putnam—a somewhat disillusioned volunteer in the French and Indian War who became a seasoned and capable leader in the Revolutionary War. A self-made man, Putnam achieved distinction during the Revolutionary War by his ingenuity and expertness as a military engineer. He was born in Sutton, Massachusetts in 1738 and was a descendant of one of the earliest settlers of Salem. According to the survey system advocated by this man who had earned the trust and confidence of Washington, acquired lands were to be divided in accordance with the New England idea of parallels of latitude and meridians of longitude. Congress tendered Putnam the offer of appointment as Government Surveyor but he declined suggesting his trusted friend, General Benjamin Tupper, be given the appointment. Tupper accepted and his surveyors gathered at Fort Pitt to begin survey of the "Seven Ranges."

In starting the survey of the Seven Ranges, a "Geographer's Line" or base line was run 42 miles due west from where the Ohio River intersects the Pennsylvania boundary and then other lines were run due south six miles apart to the Ohio River. United States geographer Thomas Hutchins is given much of the credit by many for originating the plan of dividing public lands into tracts six miles square called townships which were then subdivided into sections containing 640 acres.

Although the Ordinance of 1785 made provisions for the survey of the territory northwest of the Ohio River, and provided for ascertaining the mode of disposing of lands in this vast region, it made no provisions for government of the area. In a letter from George Washington to a congressman from New York, the veteran surveyor roughly mapped out the present states of Ohio and Michigan and offered suggestions for management of both the Indians and the settlers he expected to populate the area. But despite the fact the Seven Ranges were surveyed and the land offered for sale under the provisions of the Ordinance of 1785, little land was sold and the attempt proved a failure for all practical purposes.

The Ordinances of 1784 and 1785 lacked the desirable ingredients found in the Ordinance of 1787 which outlined an American policy for colonization of the Northwest Territory.

CHAPTER 6

The Ohio Company of Associates

"Small affairs do affect history sometimes."

Recognizing the great potential of the western lands, General Rufus Putnam had been instrumental in getting the Newburgh Petition before Congress June 16, 1783 and in April of the following year he solicited George Washington's influential assistance. Washington was extremely interested in the land project being promoted by his trusted friend and gave it the benefit of his influence to the end that on July 4, 1784 Congress directed the Paymaster General to adjust the accounts between the government and the Revolutionary War veterans and give "Continental Certificates" of the sum which might appear on such settlements as the Superintendent of Finance might direct.

The 47 year old retired Brigadier General Putnam had followed these developments closely and the enterprising engineer, who had been surveying in nearby Maine, greeted with enthusiasm the return from Pittsburgh on January 9, 1786 his old friend General Benjamin Tupper. Both men dreamed of a settlement in the area northwest of the Ohio River and had been constant confidants regarding the potential of the region. Together at Rutland, Massachusetts—often referred to as "the cradle of Ohio"—the two men conceived a plan to fill the area north and west of the Ohio with settlers and on January

25, 1786, a Massachusetts newspaper announced their invitation to meet in Boston to form an organization for that purpose.

In response to this "clarion call," a meeting was held at the "Bunch Of Grapes Tavern" in Boston on March 1, 1786. Most of those who answered the call had been signers of the Newburgh Petition and now Putnam explained the object of forming an association was to raise a fund in continental certificates for the purpose of buying land and making a settlement in the northwest country. A committee consisting of Putnam, Reverend Manasseh Cutler, Colonel John Brooks, Major Winthrop Sargent, and Captain Thomas Cushing was appointed to draft a plan of association. Just two days later another meeting was held and a stock company formed with a proposed capital of one million dollars of continental certificates with the fund to be used to purchase land northwest of the Ohio River.

The company was to be called the "Ohio Company of Associates" and Putnam was elected chairman with Winthrop Sargent to be clerk. One thousand shares of stock were to be authorized with no one to hold more than five or less than one share. Each share was to cost one thousand dollars of continental certificates and ten dollars of gold or silver to be used to defray expenses. Putnam, Cutler, and General Samuel Holden Parsons were appointed directors to manage the affairs of the company—later General James Mitchell Varnum, born at Dracut, Massachusetts in 1749 and graduate of Brown University with honors, was also named a director and Colonel Richard Platt was elected treasurer. Harvard graduate Samuel Parsons is credited by some as the one who suggested to Samuel Adams he call the first Continental Congress in 1774.

Many attending the early March meetings were charter members of an organization called the "Society Of The Cincinnati" so named because the Revolutionary War veterans thought they resembled the Roman general and statesman, Lucius Quinctius Cincinnatus, in leaving their farms and work to fight for their country. General Washington was instrumental in forming the Society which included both American as well as French officers. One of the French officers was Marie Joseph Paul Yves Roch Gilbert du Motier, the Marquis de

Lafayette (1757-1834), soldier and statesman who spent much of his own personal wealth fighting in the American Revolution and won the respect of both his comrades and the citizens of the colonies. Lafayette came to America in 1777 bringing soldier-adventurers at his own expense and Congress made him a Major General—he became a close friend of General Washington. Lafayette was a charter member of the Society Of The Cincinnati and today a chapter of this organization maintain their office in Paris near the intersection of Raspail and St. Germain Boulevards.

Lafayette died May 20, 1834 and his grave in Paris was covered with earth from Bunker Hill. There is a story told about General John Joseph Pershing's arrival in France during World War I as the commander of the American Expeditionary Forces. "Black Jack" Pershing, so called because he once commanded Negro troops, is reported to have visited the tomb of Lafayette in Paris where he laid a wreath on it proclaiming:

"Lafayette, we are here!"

This respectful act symbolized the repayment of the assistance Lafayette and his French comrades had given during the Revolutionary War. Actually, the phrase was the last sentence of a short speech made by Colonel Charles E. Stanton, who spoke for General Pershing on that occasion.

With formation of the Ohio Company of Associates the subscription books were opened and by the end of 1786 a sufficient number of shares had been subscribed to justify further proceedings. On March 8, 1787 another meeting was held in Boston and Manasseh Cutler was selected as agent of the Company to make a contract with Congress for a tract of land in what they referred to as "The Great Western Territory Of The Union." Despite the fact only 250 shares of stock had been subscribed by the spring of 1787, the optimistic Company proposed to purchase a tract of 1,500,000 acres.

Although Thomas Jefferson was in Paris at the time, it is interesting to note one historian says it was this future President's suggestion which prompted Congress to establish in 1785 the decimal system of coinage with dollars as the unit and the following year provided for issue of the gold eagle and half eagle monetary pieces. People were slow however to give up the pound, shilling, and the pence—the dollar was equal to six shillings. The Ohio Company of Associates proposed to pay for the petitioned land with Continental Certificates and because these public securities were worth only about twelve cents on the dollar, the actual purchase price was eight or nine cents an acre.

The Ohio Company of Associates formed in 1786 is not to be confused with the original "Ohio Company" organized several decades earlier in connection with land interest in the Ohio valley by prominent men of Virginia. Among the members of that early colonial company were Augustine and Lawrence Washington, elder half brothers of the future president of the United States. This grand scheme to colonize the western country was conceived in 1749 and Christopher Gist, a man who spoke half a dozen Indian dialects with fluency and knew the red man's customs, left Virginia October 31, 1750 as their representative to explore the Ohio valley as far west as the Falls (Louisville). Together with an Irishman, George Croghan, and a man of mixed blood named Andrew Montour, the expedition left the mouth of the Muskinghum in February of 1751 and explored the Miami River region. These representatives of English interests met members of the Miami, Shawnee, Delaware, and Wyandot villages and submitted glowing reports regarding the potential of the area. It will be remembered that Captain Celeron had only recently passed through the same region carrying the flag of King Louis XV of France.

The Ohio Company of Associates organized in 1786 was composed largely of Revolutionary War officers who hoped to establish homes in the western country and ultimately to found a new state. In their request for the purchase of land they made stipulations for law and order, for education, and for the maintenance of religious freedom. The total exclusion of slavery was to form an essential and irrevocable part of the constitution of the envisioned state beyond the Ohio River. The thoughts and influence of the Company's most active promoter, Rufus Putnam, is seen throughout the origin of the Ohio Company of Associates and passage of legislation to facilitate action on their petition.

But in addition to Putnam, Manasseh Cutler's ability as an agent before Congress was instrumental in the passage of the Ordinance of

1787 and favorable action on the Company's petition. Armed with some fifty letters of introduction from men who had fought and thought a new nation into potential greatness, the affable Reverend Cutler left his home in Ipswich north of Boston Sunday, June 24, 1787. He preached that day in Lynn, Massachusetts and arrived in New York where the stately and elegant agent on July 5, 1787 made an impassioned plea before Congress on behalf of the Ohio Company of Associates.

Born on a farm near Killingly, Connecticut May 13, 1742, Manasseh Cutler graduated from Yale in 1761. He was a teacher, preacher (ordained at Ipswich September 11, 1771), physician, and scientist. He served his country in the early days of the Revolutionary War as a chaplain. Because of his honesty, noble character, and fidelity to duty, men came to love and respect him knowing their interests would be safe in his hands. It was after the Revolutionary War that Cutler studied medicine and received his M.D. degree which served him well in the summer of 1788 when he visited his colleagues at Marietta and administered medicine to the sick there.

Reverend Cutler's commanding presence before Congress that early day in July of 1787 drew the attention of the delegates who were stimulated into great activity when they heard he proposed to buy land in the territory northwest of the Ohio River—the land was for sale and Congress needed the money to pay the national debt. Cutler lost no time in becoming acquainted with the various representatives and seized every opportunity to point out the advantages which would flow from consumation of the proposed legislation which would facilitate his Company's purchase petition. The wise and knowledgeable Cutler emphasized how Congress could not only pay a large percentage of the national debt but pointed out how a favorable statute would open up the vast northwest country to settlement and establish a barrier between the western Indians and the older settlements at no expense to the young government. The busy agent made himself available and agreeable to the various state representatives who had been appointed to formulate a proposed Ordinance, particularly those from the south.

On the 9th of July Congress appointed a new committee, composed of five men including Colonel Edward Carrington and Nathan Dane of Massachusetts and Richard Henry Lee of Virginia, to review the initially proposed Ordinance and prepare a frame of government for the new territory. The new committee immediately solicited Reverend Cutler's suggestions and meaningful changes were proposed by the polite but adamant agent—the proposed provisions of the Ordinance were intimately related to the interest of the Ohio Company of Associates.

Confident of success, Manasseh Cutler departed New York for Philadelphia on the afternoon of July 10th and visited with eighty-four year old Benjamin Franklin the evening of July 13, 1787—the day Congress passed the Ordinance of Freedom in New York. Cutler greeted the news with a deep sense of inner satisfaction. He had skillfully employed his knowledge as a graduate of the so-called learned professions—law, divinity, and medicine—together with an understanding of his fellow man's diverse interests in promoting the plan which was favorable to the interests of both the Ohio Company of Associates and humanity. Through Manasseh Cutler's determination and capabilities the Ordinance of 1787 irrevocably fixed the character of the immigration and determined the social, political, industrial, educational, and religious institutions of the Northwest Territory—he could be justifiably proud.

Except for Benjamin Franklin, Reverend Cutler may have been one of the fittest men on the continent for that mission of delicate diplomacy which was a must in those days of varied interests and compromise. Later Cutler declined a judgeship of the Supreme Court of the Northwest Territory offered by President Washington in 1795 and still later he became a member of the Massachusetts legislature. From 1800 to 1803 he served as a representative in Congress from his Massachusetts district. Although he did not choose to become one of the pioneer settlers of the new territory, three of his sons did join the westward movement. Manasseh Cutler died July 28, 1803 at Hamilton, Massachusetts.

It is obvious the interests of the Ohio Company of Associates and the Ordinance of 1787 were intimately related. There was also much common interest between Congress and the enterprising

Company and it was to be expected the application for purchase of land would be processed expeditiously. Congress realized the purchase was to be paid for with continental certificates but this would redeem the pledges of Congress to the army to that extent and thereby reduce the public debt. The long range plan for the colony west of the Ohio River, primarily made up of many educated men possessing the best qualities of the people of New England and the army, was felt to be a guarantee of the successful establishment of a new state in the future. Thus, the Magna Carta of the Northwest and the petition for the purchase of land by Reverend Cutler on behalf of the Ohio Company of Associates and those he represented, were parts of a single endeavor and neither would probably have occurred—or succeeded—without the other.

For all practical purposes, the contract with the Ohio Company of Associates was a multiple-purchase action with the two primary petitions being one for Cutler's Company and the other for William Duer, Secretary of the United States Board of Treasury, and his associates of the Scioto Company. Various leading persons who held government certificates proposed to make Cutler their agent and he skillfully played his offer to satisfy five million dollars of public debts through his plan—Congress could see not only opportunity to reduce the public debt but the enhancement of the value of federal lands.

The conscientious and frugal law makers of 1787 would have been appalled at talk of an annual government spending deficit of two hundred billion dollars 200 years later and, much like most of their descendants, would have been unable to fathom the enormity of a public debt exceeding two trillion dollars—a two thousand billions dollar figure which staggers the imagination of even the most learned numbers-oriented mind of the Twentieth Century.

Following the passage of the Ordinance of 1787, and empowered to negotiate a contract, on July 24, 1787 Manasseh Cutler submitted his "terms" to the Board of Treasury indicating the government was to survey the tract of land at its expense and dictated the terms of payment. The land was to be purchased at one dollar an acre less one-third off to cover the cost of bad lands and expenses incident to the surveying. One section in each township was to be reserved for support of the ministry. In the case of the Ohio Company of Associates' petition for one and a half million acres, five hundred thousand dollars was to be paid in continental certificates when the contract was signed and the remainder paid when the land survey was completed.

With such stringent terms as proposed by Cutler, his capable lobbying efforts were sorely taxed and he enlisted the aid of Colonel William Duer and Major Winthrop Sargent in contacts with their influential friends and associates. Although the initiators of the undertaking had envisioned Samuel Parsons as the first governor of the Northwest Territory, it became known the President of the Congress—Arthur St. Clair—desired the position and the shrewd Cutler met with him and "arranged" his influence. On the 27th of July Congress directed the Board of Treasury "to take order and close the contract." Sargent, heir apparent to appointment as Secretary of the Northwest Territory, was authorized to sign the contract and Manasseh Cutler left for Massachusetts where his elated colleagues listened to his report.

The contract was not formally executed until October 27, 1787 with the land tract to be bounded on the east by the Seven Ranges, on the south by the Ohio River, on the west by the 17th Range, and to extend far enough north to include areas reserved for support of schools, the ministry, a university, and land for the future disposition by Congress. The cost of the land was to be sixty-six and two-thirds cents an acre and paid for in the United States certificates of debt.

The final survey showed the tract of land contained 1,781,700 acres but because of unforeseen expenses the Ohio Company of Associates could not pay the second installment and the land patents issued on May 20, 1792 to Messrs Cutler, Putnam, Robert Oliver, and Griffin Greene—and signed by President Washington on behalf of the United States—reduced the sale to 1,064,285 acres. This final settlement included 750,000 acres (one half of the purchase) plus 214,285 acres added by Congress to be paid for with army warrants and an additional 100,000 acres which were to be divided into one hundred acre plots and given as a bounty to settlers who actually settled these "Donation Tracts" within five years and as provided for in an Act of Congress passed April 21, 1792. In accordance with Cutler's request, section sixteen in each township was reserved for the support of free schools and section twenty-nine was reserved for religious purposes. Sections eight, eleven, and twenty-six in each township were reserved for such purpose as might, in the future, be determined by Congress.

Although the agreement under which the Ohio Company of Associates was formed provided for the issue of one thousand shares, only eight hundred twenty-two were actually subscribed. Thus, each shareholder received 1,173.37 acres in seven allotments of eight acres, three acres, a house lot of .37 acres, one hundred sixty acres, one hundred acres, a six hundred forty acre section, and two hundred sixty-two acres.

As agent for the Ohio Company of Associates, Manasseh Cutler had carefully avoided any entangling alliance with the Scioto Company and only agreed to the joint purchase because of the quantity of land represented by such joint undertaking. The Scioto Company's proposed three and a half million acre purchase lay to the north and west of the Ohio Company's tract—the subsequent survey showed it contained 4,901,480 acres. It was an enormous tract of land and of great value but beset by problems as history would record.

William Duer, Secretary of the Board of Treasury, had approached Reverend Cutler with their plan to purchase land and the wise agent used the larger plan of purchase to secure passage of the Ordinance of 1787. The Scioto Company sent Joel Barlow, a man of questionable business judgment, to France where he engaged an unscrupulous character named William Playfair to sell land to the fear-worn French citizens. In a sales modus operandi which would equal the "time-share condominium" marketing of the Twentieth Century real estate speculators, Playfair dazzled the intrigued Frenchmen proclaiming:

"Fabulous Gallipolis along La Belle Riviere awaits you!"

Gallipolis, "The city of the French," was touted as the Garden of Eden where nature provided the necessities of life without labor.

"Custard grows on trees (paw paws) and candles (cat tails) are found growing in the swamps" were but two of the sales lures dangled before the naive Frenchmen who came to Alexandria, Virginia only to learn the Scioto Company did not have clear title to the land they had bought and paid for.

One French land buyer was Francois D'Hebecourt, a boyhood friend of Napoleon Bonaparte who had considered coming to America. With D'Hebecourt's reports of the villany of the Scioto Company, Bonaparte apparently changed his intention of setting up an empire in the New World. Napoleon's reaction at the treatment of his countrymen may have influenced his decision in 1803 in selling the Louisiana Territory to the United States for about $15,000,000—by that action 875,000 square miles were added to the area of the United States.

The fraudulence of the agent of the Scioto Company was embarrassing to the United States who remembered the assistance France had provided during the Revolutionary War. Through the intervention of President Washington, William Duer agreed to transport the 500 French "land owners" to their lands opposite the mouth of the Big Kanawha River which surveyors found lay within the purchase of the Ohio Company of Associates. Duer contracted with Rufus Putnam to erect some shelter for the settlers and Major John Burnham with 48 men quickly put up four rows of 20 cabins in each with blockhouses at the four corners. To these crude dwellings in the wilderness country along the Ohio River, on October 20, 1790, came the artisans, jewelers, physicians, dressmakers, servants, and the exiled nobility of France fleeing the impending French revolution and ignorant of pioneer ways. Those who remained bought their land a second time in December of 1795 from the Ohio Company of Associates at one dollar and twenty-five cents an acre. By an Act of Congress March 3, 1795 the embarrassed United States granted the remaining settlers twenty-four thousand acres of land in Scioto County east of where Portsmouth, Ohio stands today—few accepted the offer.

Incarcerated in 1792, William Duer was destined to die in prison in 1799.

CHAPTER 7

Ordinance of Freedom

"The ayes have it. Let the record show the Congress approves the Ordinance of 1787."

Arthur St. Clair
President of Congress

While some of the wisest men of the fledgling nation, held together under the Articles of Confederation, toiled in Philadelphia to draft a Constitution, in New York City fifty-five far-sighted men were at the same time writing the Ordinance of 1787 which was passed by Congress among its last acts under the Articles of Confederation.

One of the "fruits" of the Revolutionary War, this "Ordinance of Freedom" provided for establishment of the Northwest Territory sans slavery and with unique provisions for education of its populace. It provided a plan for the government of the country northwest of the Ohio River and laid the ground work for social and political democracy in the virgin forests inhabited by a red-skinned people who grew more hostile as the land-hungry "white invaders" relentlessly moved west from the Allegheny Mountains building their forts and cabins and driving the hated "land stakes" in the revered earth.

This great Magna Carta of the Northwest embodied six articles of compact between the original states and the people and states to be made out of the new territory. America could now move westward under a law of highest hope and modern ideals. Speaking as

35

handsomely as he dressed and looked, President of the Congress Arthur St. Clair smiled his approval on Friday, July 13, 1787, as he declared:

"The ayes have it!"

Born in Thurso on the northern coast of Scotland, and a Revolutionary War veteran who had served under General Washington's command, Arthur St. Clair was pleased with the wisdom of the provisions of the Charter which created a territory out of a vast wilderness founded on the principles of all men's right of life, liberty, and the pursuit of happiness. Although some would later say the appointment was not one of his choice, others would indicate St. Clair had fond hopes he might be selected as the first Governor of the Northwest Territory which was to be governed by the provisions of the Ordinance of Freedom promulgated in 1787.

Arthur St. Clair had no way of knowing it would be just four years and four months later when the army under his command would be soundly defeated along the banks of the Wabash deep in the wilderness of the Northwest Territory where Fort Recovery, Ohio would later stand. It was this disastrous carnage which sent a wave of alarm throughout the young nation and prompted President Washington to initiate the first congressional investigation in the history of the United States.

The historic Ordinance of 1787 gave attention to the matters of title to property, the disposition of estates, and included provisions regarding wills and property deeds to insure legal title to real estate could be established. Congress had power to appoint a governor and three judges who would exercise supreme executive, legislative, and judicial powers of the Northwest Territory until the people of the area were capable of self- government. A secretary was also to be appointed—later the secretary's authority was greatly expanded. The governor was to be commander-in-chief of the Northwest Territory militia.

The Ordinance of Freedom provided that a representative legislature be chosen by the people as soon as there should be five thousand free adult male inhabitants in the district with one member being allowed for each five hundred population. This state of partial self-government could be terminated when the population of the territory should equal 60,000 free inhabitants and at that time the district concerned could be admitted to the Union "on an equal footing with the original states in all respects whatever." Six "Articles of Compact" were made a part of the Ordinance of 1787 and were stated in language that clearly reflected the intent of the framers.

Typical of the many laudatory remarks voiced by noted statesmen, jurists, and educators concerning this Magna Carta of the Northwest Territory were the words of President Abraham Lincoln:

"The Ordinance of 1787 was constantly looked to whenever a new territory was to become a state. Congress always traced their course by that Ordinance."

Four decades later it was President Theodore Roosevelt who said:

"In truth the Ordinance of 1787 was so wide reaching in its effects, was drawn in accordance with so lofty a morality and such far seeing statesmanship, and was fraught with such weal for the nation, that it will ever rank among the foremost of American State papers."

During his long tenure of office (1933-1945) as President of the United States, Franklin D. Roosevelt declared:

"...with respect to that third great charter—the Northwest Ordinance. The principles therein embodied served as the highway, broad and safe, over which poured the westward march of our civilization. On this plan was the United States built."

During an address in Cincinnati, Ohio in 1837, Judge Timothy Walker praised the language of the Ordinance of Freedom saying:

37

"It approaches as nearly to absolute perfection as anything to be found in the legislation of mankind, for after the experience of fifty years it would perhaps be impossible to alter without marring it. In short, it is one of those matchless specimens of sagacious forecast which even the reckless spirit of innovation would not venture to assail."

Summarizing his research effort to trace the origin of the Ordinance of 1787, Peter Force stated in 1847:

"It has been distinguished as one of the greatest monuments of civil jurisprudence."

The loquacious Daniel Webster said no one single law of any law-giver has produced effects of more lasting character than this historic document. Before the United States Senate in 1830 he said with great eloquence:

"We are accustomed to praise the law-givers of antiquity; we help to perpetuate the fame of Solon and Lycurgus; but I doubt whether one single law of any law-giver, ancient or modern, has produced effects of more distinct, marked, and lasting character than the Ordinance of 1787. We see its consequences at this moment, and we shall never cease to see them, perhaps, while the Ohio shall flow!"

In an address at the University of Michigan on June 27, 1878 George V.N. Lothrop, L.L.D., stated:

"In advance of the coming millions, it had, as it were, shaped the earth and the heavens of the sleeping empire. The Great Charter of the Northwest had consecrated it irrevocably to human freedom, to religion, learning, and free thought. This one act is the most dominant one in our history, since the landing of the Pilgrims. It is the act that became decisive in the Great Rebellion. Without it, so far as human judgment can discover, the victory of free labor would have been impossible."

Authorship of legislation which achieves greatness is usually a matter for later controversy. As previously discussed, legislation to provide for the government of the new territory had been before the Congress for several years before 1787 and in the deliberations the anti-slavery question had been an important issue. Thomas Jefferson has been liberally extolled as the architect of the Ordinance of 1787, particularly as regards the cause which prohibits slavery and involuntary servitude. The provisos for education are also often attributed to Jefferson's wise statesmanship and unselfish patriotism but General Rufus Putnam was also vitally interested in the inclusion of provisions for education of the new territory's populace and his thoughts were a basic tenet of the undertaking by the Ohio Company of Associates.

As mentioned previously herein, after many changes of the provisions of a proposed statute—and many in the final few days just preceding passage—the Ordinance of 1787 in its final form was passed by Congress and envisioned government built primarily for man, rather than man for the government. It forever prohibited slavery in the Northwest Territory and the Ordinance submitted came from a committee of five, three of whom were southern delegates. It was passed by a vote of five southern and two northern states. The vote on this statute gave rise to the later claim by some states that the Ordinance of 1787 was unconstitutional since it was not agreed on by all of the states as required by the Articles of Confederation.

Charles King, president of Columbia College at one time, published a paper in 1855 claiming his father (Rufus King) was the author of the non-slavery provision of this historic document. And George Lothrop, speaking at the University of Michigan in 1878, attributed the education provisions of the Ordinance of 1787 to the wisdom of Nathan Dane saying:

"It was a graduate of Harvard, who, in 1787, when framing the Great Charter for the Northwest, had consecrated it irrevocably to Human Freedom, to Religion,

Learning, and Free Thought. It was the proud boast of Themistocles, that he knew how to make a small city of a great state. Greater than his was the wisdom and prescience of Nathan Dane, who knew how to take the pledges of the future, and to snatch from the wilderness and inviolable Republic of Free Labor and Free Thought."

In a speech delivered by Daniel Webster before the Senate in 1830, he gave to Nathan Dane of Massachusetts the entire credit for devising the Ordinance of 1787. Thomas H. Benton, in a rebuttal speech, countered by declaring:

"He (Daniel Webster) has brought before us a certain Nathan Dane, of Beverly, Massachusetts, and loaded him with such an exuberance of blushing honors as no modern name has been known to merit or claim. So much glory was caused by a single act, and that act the supposed authorship of the Ordinance of 1787, and especially the clause in it which prohibits slavery and involuntary servitude. So much encomium and such greatful consequences it seems a pity to spoil, but spoilt it must be; for Mr. Dane was no more the author of that Ordinance, sir, than you or I ... that Ordinance, and especially the non-slavery clause, was not the work of Nathan Dane of Massachusetts, but of Thomas Jefferson of Virginia."

In 1876 William F. Poole published a treatise in the "North American Review" wherein he portrays Dr. Manasseh Cutler as the chief architect of the Ordinance of 1787 in a convincing manner. Poole even questions whether Thomas Jefferson was actually the architect of the Ordinance of 1784 saying it was almost identical to a plan submitted by David Howell of Rhode Island in 1783. But regardless of credit for authorship, it was Chief Justice Salmon Portland Chase (1808-1873), noted jurist and twice elected Republican governor of Ohio, who said of this Charter:

"Never, probably, in the history of the world, did a measure of legislation so accurately fulfill, and yet so mightily exceed, the anticipations of the legislators. The Ordinance has well been described as having been a pillar of cloud by day and a fire by night in the settlement and government of the Northwestern states."

Of Judge Salmon P. Chase, whose portrait appears on the U.S. $10,000 bill, President Lincoln once said:

"Chase is one and a half times bigger than any other man I ever knew!"

Statutes such as the Ordinance of 1787 are seldom the work of one person, indeed, research indicates this great document was the result of the coordinated efforts of many whose thoughts were finally reduced to this compromise legislation. Any examination of this great charter requires a review of the multi-faceted "trail" which led to its promulgation. Inextricably interwoven in the formulation, adoption, and implementation of the Ordinance of Freedom were the efforts and thoughts of a number of individuals, many of whom endured the danger and hardships of travel through Pennsylvania and down the Ohio to the "promised land" envisioned by the men who signed the Newburg Petition years earlier.

Examination of the provisions of the Ordinance of 1787, included herein (page 87) for reference purpose, will show this important and historic document contains two principal parts. The first describes the actual scheme of the government to be erected and the second part contains the six articles declared to be a "compact" between the people of the original states and the people and "states of the Territory of the United States Northwest of the River Ohio." These six articles were to "forever remain unalterable" unless changed by common consent. In unmistakeable language Article I guarantees freedom of religion while Article II insures the inhabitants of the territory will be entitled to the benefits of the writ of habeas corpus and trial by jury. With respect to the all important right of contracts, Article II states:

"...in the just preservation of rights and property, it is understood and declared that no law ought ever to be made, or have force in the said territory, that shall, in any manner whatever, interfere with or affect private contracts or engagements bona fide and without fraud, previously formed."

As soon as the Ordinance of 1787 was adopted by Congress it was sent to the Constitutional Convention in Philadelphia where some of its provisions were embodied in that landmark undertaking. For example, paragraph 1, section 10, of Article 1 of the Constitution prohibits a state from passing any law impairing the obligation of contracts.

While the Ordinance of 1787 made no specific provision for public school lands, it laid the basis for education in the Northwest Territory by its declaration for the encouragement of schools and outside the formal tenets of law a public land policy made our public schools and university education system an integral and distinctive feature of the government. Much thought was obviously given to the details of government of the new territory and for its settlement in such manner as would best promote the individual and of the future republic. Article II is explicit in its declaration:

"Religion, morality, and knowledge, being necessary to good government and the happiness of mankind, schools and the means of education shall forever be encouraged."

In the contract of October 27, 1787 with the Ohio Company of Associates, Congress agreed to give two townships of land for "the uses of a university." After the Treaty of Greene Ville in 1795, these townships were identified and early in the 19th century the legislature of the Northwest Territory passed an act establishing a university at Athens—it was the first legislation passed in the new territory for the advancement of higher education. Founded in 1804, Ohio University was the first state university in the world under democratic government. Each of the states formed from the territory created by the Ordinance of 1787 now maintain a university at public expense.

Although some of the unfortunate developments reported in the history of the Northwest Territory might indicate no thought was given the Indians, the framers of the Ordinance of Freedom had given a great deal of thought to the red man's plight and—praying the doctrine of the Golden Rule would be followed—provided in Article III:

"The utmost good faith shall always be observed toward the Indians."

Language can not make a more emphatic declaration and it was intended to put into practice the morality and justice the framers of the Ordinance meant to teach by providing for the security of the land and property of the Indians, and for laws— founded in humanity and right—to protect the red man in every way and prevent wrongs being done them. Unfortunately, the intent of this proviso became clouded in the ensuing conflict with the Indians.

Article IV provided not only for the taxation of the inhabitants of the various states formed from the Territory but declared states formed from the Northwest Territory would forever remain a party of this confederacy of United States. This provision was often cited when the storm clouds of the Civil War rolled over the Northwest Territory seventy four years later and the Ohio River became the basic line of federal defense in the western country east of the Mississippi River.

Although Article V sparked heated debate when the boundaries of some of the states were defined by Congress, the Ordinance of 1787 was specific in stating not less than three nor more than five states were to be created from the Northwest Territory. To no avail some of the states argued the Ordinance of 1787 was unconstitutional because it had been approved by only eight states instead of the nine required for passage under the Articles of Confederation

It was Article VI which clearly stated there should be neither slavery nor involuntary servitude in the Territory. Advocates of slavery made strenuous efforts to secure its introduction when Ohio was admitted to the Union but they failed. As with the Indiana Territory's similar request, Congress firmly maintained the Articles of Compact. Without this provision Illinois and Indiana might have joined the Union as slave states. In 1802 General William Henry Harrison, then governor of the Indiana Territory, hosted a convention to consider means by which slavery could be introduced into the Territory. A congressional committee, chaired by John Randolph of Virginia, reported to Congress adversely:

"The increasing population of the State of Ohio evinces in the opinion of your committee, that the labor of slaves is not necessary to promote the growth and settlement of colonies in that region. The committee deems it dangerous and inexpedient to impair a provision of the Articles of Compact wisely calculated to promote the happiness and prosperity of the northwestern country."

It is interesting to note most of the humanitarian provisions of the Ordinance of Freedom adopted by Congress in 1787 became part of the Constitution in the first amendments to the Constitution in 1791. One of the great provisos found its way into our organic law seventy-eight years later when slavery was abolished by the 13th Amendment December 18, 1865.

Thus, a fledgling government "of the people, by the people, for the people" first found concrete expression in the Ordinance of 1787 and its enlightened provisions materially aided the growth of the country and its development from a union of thirteen seaboard states into the vast nation it is today. The guidance of this Charter attracted the New Englanders, the Dutch and Germans from Pennsylvania, and the conscientious settlers of Virginia and the Carolinas. The sturdy pioneers of Kentucky wandered north and even the light-hearted French immigrants who remained contributed to the "melting pot" of the Northwest Territory. Representatives of the diverse and important segments of the early colonies provided the Northwest Territory with a "Magna Carta" which proved workable and withstood attempts to alter its provisions. Guided by the provisions of the Ordinance of Freedom, the determination and undaunted spirit

44

of our pioneer settlers made the Northwest Territory the political and industrial heart of the nation.

CHAPTER 8

The Constitution

"We the people of the United States, in order to form a more perfect Union, establish justice, insure domestic tranquility, provide for the common defense, promote the general welfare, and secure the blessings of liberty to ourselves and our posterity, do ordain and establish this Constitution for the United States of America."

By unanimous consent of those assembled at Philadelphia for the Constitutional Convention, on September 17, 1787 twelve states approved the proposed Constitution—ratification of the statute by nine of the twelve states represented at the convention was required for establishment of the unifying government. In accordance with one of the compromise agreements, the first ten amendments to the Constitution, eight of which are known as the "Bill of Rights," were proposed September 25, 1789 and have been in force since December 15, 1791.

With assurance a bill of rights would be included, on December 7, 1787 Delaware became the first state to ratify the Constitution and Pennsylvania and New Jersey followed the same month. Georgia became the fourth state to ratify in 1788 followed the same year by Connecticut, Massachusetts, Maryland, and South Carolina. On the 21st of June in 1788 New Hampshire, the northernmost of the thirteen original states, ratified as the ninth state and the Constitution became the supreme law of the United States. Virginia ratified as the tenth state on June 25, 1788 and New York did likewise the next month. With North Carolina's ratification in 1789 and Rhode Island adding its approval in 1790, all of the thirteen original colonies were now members of the United States. Vermont ratified in 1791 as the fourteenth state to do so.

It had been a trying period, and the ratified Constitution was the epitome of compromise, but the United States of America had a unifying charter—a government deriving its just powers from the consent of the governed as envisioned by the signatories to the Declaration of Independence. But while the Ordinance of Freedom was being promulgated in July of 1787, Patrick Henry, Samuel Adams, and several others were examining the proposed Constitution with a certain amount of suspicion asking:

"Where are the inalienable rights of men set forth in the Declaration of Independence?"

In accordance with a consensus agreement of the representatives from five states who met in Annapolis, Maryland in 1786, and at the urging by delegates from Virginia in particular, delegates from all states were invited to a Constitutional Convention in Philadelphia. On May 25, 1787 the delegates from all states except Rhode Island gathered and George Washington was elected President of the Convention which then took up the arduous task of drafting a charter agreeable to all—a monumental task.

Divided as the representatives may have been, one thing they did agree on—any westward colonization would produce the inevitable "land grabbing schemes" and various plans had been advocated to discourage this undesirable possibility. The Ordinance of 1784 had attempted to provide a plan for the western country but it lacked universal support and, despite a tacit understanding they would do so, in 1784 Massachusetts and Connecticut had not ceded their charter claims to the central government. The Land Ordinance of 1785 said nothing about the laws to go with the land—it lacked too much to succeed.

Peletiah Webster had proposed township surveys and sale of the western lands in plots small enough to prevent land speculation—the plan provided a semblance of orderly growth through sale of one range at a time. Although there was merit in Webster's proposal, and that of several others, Congress knew the government had—for all practical purposes—only in effect a quit claim deed from Great Britian to the land north and west of the Ohio River. The "rights" of the Indians had to be quieted if the settlers were to live in peace in the Northwest Territory.

During the period following the end of the Revolutionary War there had been increasing talk among the various state representatives of a unifying constitution but, in addition to some of the state's deep-rooted feeling of loss with the surrender of their charter claim, there was the undeniable rights of the Indians of the region north and west of the Ohio River which had to be quieted by purchase or conquest and this prompted considerable oratorical comment and debate among the voice-gifted state representatives.

Some of the state representatives pointed to their "sacrifice" in ceding charter claims to the central government—these independent-prone states were interested in the opportunities of westward expansion. Maryland, whose charter claims were limited, had led the cry that all western lands were won by a common effort and the territory should of right be ceded to a central government. It was a point of unity and would provide means to lessen the common debt if the land could be sold. As one representative voiced with great conviction:

"Property held in common would break down old animosities!"

Virginia's representatives did not allow anyone to forget she had sent George Rogers Clark into the western country during the Revolution and drove the British from what were ostensibly her charter lands along the Mississippi. In May of 1783 Congress had recognized Virginia's request for bounty lands north of the Ohio with the "Virginia Military Lands" and she ceded her charter claims the next year. New York had ceded claims to the western territory in 1781 but with the Treaty of Fort Stanwix (Rome, New York) concluded with the Iroquois October 22, 1784 she still nurtured thoughts of westward expansion. Massachusetts and Connecticut had kept their charter claims alive until, at Maryland's repeated insistence, they ceded their claims to the central government in 1785 and 1786.

Now, in the early summer of 1787, the delegates to the Convention in Philadelphia were reminded of the treaties concluded at Fort McIntosh and Fort Finney the past two years whereby the Indians had surrendered to the United States government their claims to much of the territory in question and many of the delegates were optimistic a unified government could handle any further difficulties in the Northwest Territory.

It is worth noting here that at the end of the Revolutionary War only 700 men remained in the army with no one having rank above that of a captain. This "military force" was subsequently reduced to 25 men stationed at Fort Pitt and fifty men at West Point. Many Revolutionary War officers were addressed using their military service rank despite the fact they had been relieved from active military duty. Such was the status of the fledgling nation's military might as the new republic representatives discussed expulsion of the British forces that remained in the Northwest Territory and conquest of the Indian inhabitants of the same region as might be necessary.

With such monumental problems confronting the young government of the Articles of Confederation, the delegates to the Constitutional Convention met behind closed doors—they represented the wealthier classes of the thirteen states for all practical purposes. It was to be expected that some preferred a limited monarchy and an aristocratic system of government. Friends of the proposed Constitution which was adopted agreed the first Congress under the new government would propose a "bill of rights" to correct some of the objectionable provisions of the document being considered. By September 17, 1787 the delegates completed, and 39 of them signed, a Constitution to present to the people for ratification—it was a compromise of some aristocratic desires to obtain a system of government but it represented the thoughts of some of the best brains in the new country and was the only frame of government that had a chance of being accepted by nine of the thirteen states which constituted the agreed upon quorum. The old and the young delegates, all weary of the weeks of debate, were confident of the document's ratification as they watched General Jonathan Dayton—youngest man to sign the Constitution—affix his signature.

The Constitution adopted by the delegates in Philadelphia gave to the government attributes and powers of nationality which it had not before possessed. The sale of land to the Ohio Company of Associates was the first complete assertion of Congress over the Northwest Territory as property and the contract was signed October 27, 1787 by Samuel Osgood and Arthur Lee as Commissioners of Public Lands on behalf of the United States Board of Treasury. Manasseh Cutler and Winthrop Sargent signed for the Ohio Company of Associates.

The first federal Congress under the Constitution met in New York on March 4, 1789 and the next month elected George Washington to be the first President of the United States and John Adams as Vice-President. Washington was inaugurated into office April 30, 1789. His Secretary of the Treasury, Alexander Hamilton, apprised him of the country's debt—$12,000,000 to foreign countries and $42,000,000 to its own people. The nation's first President would have taken small consolation, and probably have suffered apoplexy, had he by some quirk of providence been privy to the Treasury's announcement two hundred years later that the federal deficit for 1984 was *only* 175.3 billion dollars—down ten percent from the previous year.

The Constitution was a product of what has been called "the critical period of the American history" and was one of two great documents promulgated in the same time frame and going hand in hand in our great nation's heritage—the other was the Ordinance of 1787.

CHAPTER 9

"For the Ohio Country"

"They say the buckeye leaves expand,
Five-fingered as an open hand
Of love and brotherhood the sign
Be welcome! What is mine is thine!"

From "The Buckeye Tree"

The tract of land purchased by the Ohio Company of Associates was the only land the United States could really give anyone clear title. Connecticut retained claim to her Western Reserve of 3,667,000 acres to the north of the Fort McIntosh Treaty line and the land between the Scioto River and the Little Miami was under Virginia option. But, although the purchased land was not the best area for farming, it was relatively close to New England, was on the Ohio River, and was close to Fort Harmar which had been built in 1785 under Major John Doughty's direction. Thirteen families lived on the patent of Isaac Williams at Williamstown on the Virginia side of the Ohio River opposite the mouth of the Muskinghum. Thomas Hutchins, geographer of the United States, told Rufus Putnam:

"The Muskinghum Valley is the best part of the whole of the western country in my opinion!"

With the contract signed in late October of 1787, the following month the Ohio Company of Associates held a meeting at Cromwell's Head Tavern in Boston and plans were firmed

51

concerning the long journey westward. Rufus Putnam, as elected superintendent, and his associates made plans for a city at the mouth of the Muskinghum of four thousand acres with wide streets and public parks—one hundred houses were to be built on three sides of a square for reception of the settlers who would follow. The superintendent was authorized to employ four surveyors and twenty-two assistants, six boat builders, four house carpenters, one blacksmith, and nine laborers. Each man was required to furnish himself with a rifle, bayonet, six flints, powder horn and pouch, half a pound of powder, one pound of balls, and one pound of buckshot. Surveyors were to receive twenty-seven dollars a month and laborers four dollars a month and board.

So severe was the anticipated winter travel, no women were allowed to accompany the first group. Eight hundred miles in the cold winter months with a plodding ox team and over the roughest of roads along uncharted trails through the wilderness and across swollen streams was rough enough for the men let alone subjecting the women to such hardships. Despite the anticipated danger and rigor of the forthcoming journey, with undaunted enthusiasm the men cheerfully planned the trip and made such preparations as necessary. The party of forty-eight was divided into two groups for the long trek and Major Haffield White, a Revolutionary War officer, was designated to lead the first party of twenty-two.

These were men of noble purpose and action and only five weeks after the signing of the contract three volleys of gunfire greeted the New England dawn as the first party started from Cutler's home in Ipswich, Massachusetts on December 3rd. Cutler provided a wagon covered with a black canvas labeled: FOR THE OHIO COUNTRY AT MUSKINGHUM! Although Manasseh Cutler was not destined to be one of the pioneer settlers, his three sons by name of Charles, Ephraim, and Jervis did become early residents of the Northwest Territory and 19 year old Jervis was one of those who left Ipswich that morning in 1787.

The lead party proceeded to Danvers, Massachusetts where Major Haffield White and Captain Ezra Putnam assumed command and they were on their way. On January 23, 1788 this party of 22 reached Alexander Simeral's Ferry on the Youghiogheny River about

25 miles southeast of Pittsburgh where West Newton would stand years later.

One month after their departure the second party of 26 settlers assembled at Hartford, Connecticut and on January 1, 1788 "headed out" under leadership of Colonel Ebenezer Sproat who stood six feet four inches in height. This party included four surveyors and their assistants. Rufus Putnam joined this group between Harrisburg and Lebanon in Pennsylvania at Swatara Creek— he had been delayed by business at the New York war office. By previous agreement the two parties had arranged to meet at Simeral's Ferry.

In the long trip over the sometimes trackless mountains both parties had to contend with swollen, bridgeless streams and trails often hidden in the deep snow. Weaned on the hardships of the war, each party pushed on through the wilderness country seeing only the infrequent prints of buffalo or deer and occasionally those of a band of Indians. Inclement weather prompted the second party to abandon their wagons at Cooper's Tavern near the foot of the Tuscarora Mountains and Putnam ordered sledges built to traverse the snow. On they pushed over the Glades Trail and in mid-February after 45 days of having battled the elements the second party reached Simeral's Ferry which had been started in 1778 fifteen miles below Stewart's Crossing. The Putnam party was bitterly disappointed to find the first group did not have the boats ready for the downstream journey as planned—due to severe weather not a single board was ready to build the all important river craft and some of Major White's party had smallpox.

But these were determined men of steadfast purpose, many of whom had weathered the terrible winter weather at Valley Forge, and despite the adversities after six weeks of unremitting toil they were ready to embark on the river journey. With Putnam's arrival, and availability of more laborers, work had proceeded fairly rapidly under Jonathan Devol, a ship builder by trade. The largest boat was 50 feet in length, 13 feet wide, and built to carry 21 tons. Although some called it the "Adventure Galley" and others preferred to name it "The American Mayflower," in Putnam's diary he listed the boat as "The Union Galley."

In addition to this craft, a large flatboat measuring 28 by eight feet and three canoes were constructed. The canoes were two ton, one ton, and eight hundred pound burden type craft respectively and were more properly called pirogues—a log canoe shaped boat split in half lengthwise and with a wide section inserted between the two halves.

Benjamin Tupper must have given considerable thought to river travel as he and his companions labored to build the boats for their downstream journey. On August 15th, just five months later, Tupper showed General Rufus Putnam his crank turned propellor boat he had constructed at Marietta—it was a screw with short blades which Putnam noted in his diary as "a useful discovery." Thus the first screw propellor was invented in the wilds of the Northwest Territory with necessity truly being the mother of invention.

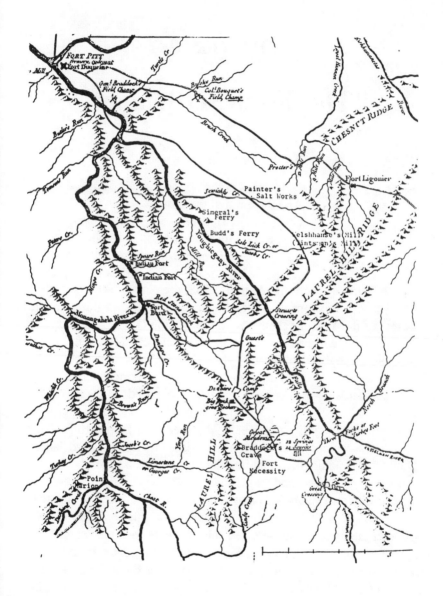

CHAPTER 10

"The First Settlement"

"The year's at the spring
And the day's at the morn,
God's in His Heaven—
All's right with the world."

Robert Browning (1812-1889)

On Tuesday morning, April 1, 1788, the pioneer settlers pushed away from the shore at Simeral's Ferry and drifted out into the waters of the Youghiogheny. With the "Union Galley" decked over and strongly constructed it led the way closely followed by the flatboat which they had named "The Adelphia." Accompanied by the three huge canoes the flotilla made a strange looking river party by later standards but it was sufficient unto their needs in the spring of 1788.

Fortunately spring came early that year and the passing vistas provided a welcome relief from the winter travel and hard labor. Down the Youghiogheny and into the Monongahela River the flotilla drifted downstream and passed the point where Fort Pitt stood majestically on a spit of land that jutted into the confluence of the two rivers which melted together to spawn the mighty Ohio River. Colonel Henry Bouquet selected this strategic location for his fort almost one hundred years after Sieur de Robert La Salle drifted down the Ohio in 1669. In 1749 Captain Celeron de Bienville of France made his way down La Belle Riviere when the French took notice of the fact the British were becoming interested in the rich fur trade they were enjoying. Now in 1788 these settlers of the United States were headed for the Northwest Territory and their spirits were high that day in early April.

The flotilla drifted by the mouth of the Beaver River less than twenty-five miles below Fort Pitt—it was the place where the Treaty of Fort McIntosh had been signed. The river party had no way of knowing it was also the place where one of the Ohio Company of Associates' directors, Judge Samuel H. Parsons, would drown less than a year later in 1789 while returning from the Western Reserve. His great spirit would take its untimely flight to the God who gave it and leave the blossoming Northwest Territory and the fledgling nation poorer in the wake of his death.

Farther downstream the flotilla passed the mouth of the Yellow Creek where Mingo Chief Logan's family was so brutally murdered by Jacob Greathouse and his evil companions on April 30, 1774. By the evening of April 4th they had reached the mouth of Buffalo Creek (now Wellsburg, West Virginia), a point on the Ohio River about 50 miles east of Gnadenhutten on the Tuscarawas where white soldiers under Colonel Williamson had bludgeoned to death and burned more than 90 Christian Delaware Indians in March of 1782. The early Moravian efforts led by Reverend David Zeisberger to christianize the Indians in Ohio was laudable and this dastardly massacre further inflamed the red man's hatred for the "white invaders."

John Mathews, at the direction of Rufus Putnam, had been working since February 27, 1788 gathering provisions at the mouth of Buffalo Creek above Wheeling. The horses, oxen, and wagons had been sent overland from Simeral's Ferry and were waiting at the mouth of Buffalo Creek. Putnam's party stopped the entire day of April 5, 1788 to load their precious cargo and soon after pushing off again they passed Wheeling. It was here that Colonel Ebenezer Zane and his sister Betty had held off an Indian and British attack in September of 1782 led by Captain Henry Bradt against Fort Henry.

On the 6th of April the flotilla tied up at Round Bottom—it was land owned by George Washington 70 miles above the mouth of the Muskinghum. That evening they bravely pushed out into the river again.

Through the light rain and mist on the morning of April 7th the anxious travelers watched the tree lined shore. Among those trees was the ever present buckeye tree which was destined to become the state tree of Ohio and the subject of a poem, "The Buckeye Tree," which would appear in "The Western Statesman," an early Lawrenceburg, Indiana newspaper. The "fruit" of the buckeye tree is a nut which resembles the eye of a male deer (buck) and the Indians called it "hetuck."

So absorbed were the settlers in watching the ever-changing misty vistas and the ghost-like trees that dipped their early spring foilage in the passing water, the flotilla started to drift right on past the mouth of the Muskinghum about mid-day. Although the dense undergrowth along the northern shore of the Ohio shielded their destination from view, the alert soldiers from Fort Harmar observed the passing craft and after hailing the party used ropes to tow the boats several hundred feet back upstream where they tied up along the shore of their new home.

Along with Major John Doughty and his troops from Fort Harmar, 70 Wyandot and Delaware Indians welcomed the 48 settlers that first Monday in April—Captain Pipe, Chief of the Delawares, was among them. The Indians graciously greeted the new arrivals, accepted the proffered gifts, and offered their pelts for trade as a feast was prepared for the pioneer settlers. But with their arrival the settlers knew there were many questions of paramount importance—shelter, food, protection against the wilderness inhabitants, assignment of land, clearing of the land plots, and planting of crops. Polite in their association, but ever wary of the Indians, the arriving settlers fell to work almost immediately.

While hearing of Major Doughty's garden near Fort Harmar and boasts of having apple trees and peach trees already growing, Rufus Putnam directed the effort of setting up his headquarters tent the afternoon of their arrival—it was a tent taken from British General John Burgoyne at Saratoga October 17, 1777 and the veteran General was justifiably proud of it. It now served its purpose well.

On the very next day the laborers began clearing the land as surveyors started to lay out the eight acre lots Putnam had planned for. By April 12th four acres had been cleared along the east bank of the Muskinghum at "The Point" as the settlers called it. The settlement was first called "Muskinghum," a form of the Delaware word "Mooskingung" meaning Elk Eye River. Manasseh Cutler had suggested for a name the Greek word "Adelphia" which means brethern. But Cutler was back in Massachusetts and on July 2, 1788 it was resolved the settlement be called Marietta—a word formed from the first and last syllables of the name of Queen Marie Antoinette of France as a tribute to those who had helped the colonial states throw off the shackles of English rule. Why the final "e" was changed to "a" is uncertain.

The beautiful Marie Antoinette, Vienna born daughter of Emperor Francis I and Marie Theresa of Austria, died on the guillotine in 1793 during the French Revolution. As wife of King Louis XVI her extravagance was well known and reportedly helped pave the way for the bloody Revolution in France. There is a story indicating she once asked one of her ministers why the people were angry and was told: "Because they have no bread." Marie Antoinette, friend of the Marquis de Lafayette and of American liberty, is said to have replied:

"Then let them eat cake!"

It is worth remembering the founding fathers of our nation eagerly accepted an alliance during the Revolutionary War with monarchical France without ever fudging their detestation of absolute monarchies in general. As some unknown sage once observed: "War makes strange bed-fellows."

There were 48 in that first party and 89 more settlers had joined the settlement by the end of the year. Many of those in the first group were members of a traveling lodge of Free Masons—the lodge had been chartered in Massachusetts in 1775. And, as previously indicated, many were also charter members of the Society Of The Cincinnati. Fifty of the pioneer settlers that first year were Revolutionary War veterans and George Washington said of them:

"No colony in America was ever settled under such favorable auspices as that which has just commenced at the Muskinghum. Information, property, and strength will be its characteristics. I know many of the settlers personally, and there never were men better calculated to promote the welfare of such a community."

New Englanders called it "Putnam's Paradise" and others referred to the Marietta settlement as "Cutler's Indian Heaven." Regardless of what it was called, the arriving settlers that first spring found the trees in leaf and grass in abundance for their horses. During his visit to Marietta that summer Reverend Cutler reported having seen "a hollow tree forty-one and a half feet in circumference that would hold eighty-four men or afford room for six horsemen to ride abreast!"

According to a report by Colonel John May, who arrived with a party of men on May 26, 1788, the growth circles of one tree indicated it to be 463 years old. Colonel May reported he was served "beef ala mode, boiled fish, bear steaks, roast venison, excellent succotash, salads, and cranberry sauce" in dinner with General Josiah Harmar. Venison sold for two cents a pound and bear meat was three cents a pound.

Other reports said, "Corn has grown nine inches in twenty-four hours" and "a hunter could kill twenty deer in a single day near Marietta and wild turkeys weigh sixteen to thirty pounds." The woods were indeed alive with foxes, opossum, raccoon, beaver, otter, rabbits, and squirrels but bears, panthers, wild cats, and wolves were a constant menace to the settler's stock. In a letter to his family back in New England one of the settlers indicated the largest fish caught was a black fish weighing ninety-six pounds and told of a pike six feet in length which weighed almost 100 pounds.

Those first few weeks at Marietta were busy days and the Ohio Company of Associates' land office was quickly erected—within its walls the early maps of the Northwest Territory were made, surveys were platted, and the sale and allotting of land carried on. The land office served as the business office and headquarters for Rufus Putnam as superintendent of the undertaking. Later, from 1796 to

1803, Putnam held the office of Surveyor-General of the United States and during that period the work of the government was done in this building. Thus, the land office at Marietta has a reverent guardianship—no other building in the Northwest Territory had so important a connection with the business purposes of the early settlers after their arrival at the mouth of the Muskinghum.

The first Marietta streets ran parallel to the Muskinghum River and were ninety feet wide—they were designated by numbers and the cross streets were named after Putnam, Washington, and other Revolutionary War generals. "The Bouery" along the river was dedicated forever as a public park. A creek which emptied into the Muskinghum near the seventy-two room stockade was named the Tiber after the river in Rome. The stockade, Campus Martius, took its name from the grassy plain along the Tiber in ancient Rome—the name means "a field dedicated to Mars, the god of war." The use of classical names indicates the cultured founders of Marietta were familiar with Latin and Greek literature.

Campus Martius was located three quarters of a mile above the Ohio River and consisted of fourteen two-story houses arranged as curtains in the form of a hollow square one hundred eighty feet on each side with a blockhouse on each corner. The upper story of the blockhouse projected beyond the wall of the lower story and was made of poplar planks four inches thick and eighteen to twenty inches wide. The northeast blockhouse served as a place for religious meeting and court and, after his arrival, the Northwest Territory secretary had his office strategically located in a room above the west gate.

In their labor of building the stockade the first year the settlers found evidence of ancient earthworks and unearthed a lead plate which had been left by Captain Celeron de Bienville in 1749 claiming the land for France. It was a fine marker but they needed the lead for bullets more than artifacts out of the past.

Despite the opportunities of the Marietta settlement, and for a variety of reasons—the Indian danger not being the least— hundreds of immigrants drifted right on by the mouth of the Muskinghum and this became a matter of concern to the Ohio Company of Associates in the winter of 1788. One year earlier, in a letter of December 9,

1787 General Harmar reported: "Since June of this year I have seen 146 boats containing 3,196 souls, 1,381 horses, 245 sheep, 171 cattle, 24 hogs, and 165 wagons pass the mouth of the Muskinghum on the way to Kentucky." On the south side of the Ohio opposite Fort Harmar Major Isaac Williams had already started his settlement called Williamstown when Putnam and his party of settlers arrived.

The "availability" of Marietta in 1788 did not halt the down- river migration and the worried directors of the Ohio Company began offering one hundred acre plots to settlers who would build a dwelling twenty four by eighteen feet within five years, plant fifty apple or pear trees and twenty peach trees within three years, cultivate five acres, and provide themselves with arms and ammunition for defense. This proved to be an expensive venture and prompted the Company to later petition Congress for land used for such donation purposes and a "Donation Tract" twenty-two by seven miles was approved.

Judge James Mitchel Varnum arrived at the mouth of the Muskinghum with forty settlers on June 5, 1788 including James Owen and his wife Mary—she was the first woman settler. Each arriving settler viewed with surprise the amount of work which had been done since the first party arrived. "By June 20th of 1788 one hundred thirty-two acres of corn had been planted in addition to large fields of beans, potatoes, and other vegetables" according to one historian.

On June 13th of that first year an informal meeting was held and the settlers named Colonel Return Jonathan Meigs to administer the laws of the settlement. With the settlement christened "Marietta" on July 2nd, two days later work was suspended to celebrate the July 4th anniversary of the Declaration of Independence. A thirteen gun salute by Fort Harmar opened the day of festivity and a table sixty feet in length was set up at "The Point" and loaded with wild meat, fish, and wine. General Harmar and his lady attended the celebration and heard Judge James Varnum's prayerful word regarding the anticipated arrival of the appointed governor, Arthur St. Clair:

"Thou gently flowing Ohio whose surface reflecteth no images but the impending Heaven, bear him safely to this anxious spot."

CHAPTER 11

Hail the Chief!

"Uneasy lies the head that wears a crown!"

From "Henry IV" by
William Shakespeare

The stately looking and knowledgeable veteran of war and government matters arrived at Fort Harmar on July 9, 1788 with his credentials as governor of the Northwest Territory. Sergeant Joseph Buell wrote in his diary that day:

"On landing he was saluted with thirteen rounds from the field piece."

The troops of Fort Harmar, dressed in their finest, paraded and music played a salute in a manner befitting the arrival of the first governor of the Northwest Territory. Claps of thunder and occasional rain accompanied his entry to Fort Harmar on the shore of the Muskinghum opposite the busy and growing settlement of Marietta.

Arthur St. Clair found himself in a congenial atmosphere and a few days later received a tremendous formal welcome by the pioneer settlers. Another gun salute was accorded St. Clair on July 15th by the Marietta settlement when the officials of the Northwest Territory were duly installed with appropriate pomp and ceremony and the first civil government west of the Allegheny Mountains was established.

On July 20, 1788 Reverend Daniel Breck delivered an inspiring sermon to a number of settlers from Marietta and the little Williamstown settlement across the Ohio River. The neighborly residents of Williamstown were helpful to the Marietta pioneer settlers in both spirit and deed. When a devastating early frost in the fall of 1789 dampened the spirits of the settlers and life was maintained to a great extent by hunting, fishing, and the gathering and storing of the wild berries and fruits which grew on the wooded slopes nearby, during the following winter Isaac and Rebecca Williams sold corn at fifty cents a bushel to their friends across the river and to the hungry down-river settlers of Columbia and Losantiville rather than accept the going rate of two dollars.

Only a week after St. Clair had been officially installed as governor, on July 21st the directors of the Ohio Company of Associates present at Marietta ordered the carpenters be paid fifty cents a day and one ration to complete the blockhouses of Campus Martius. Superintendent Putnam also announced laborers were henceforth to receive seven dollars a month and one ration per day. A ration consisted of one and a half pounds of bread or flour; one pound of pork, beef, or venison; vegetables; and one gill of whiskey.

Among the entourage accompanying St. Clair to Marietta was Judge Samuel Holden Parsons. Judge James M. Varnum had arrived in early June the previous month. Unfortunately, the judgeships of both these fine jurists and veterans of the Revolutionary War was terminated by reason of death. George Turner was appointed as Varnum's successor and Rufus Putnam was named by Congress as Parson's replacement.

Major Winthrop Sargent had been appointed by Congress as the Secretary of the Northwest Territory. The Ordinance of 1787 vested the governing authority in the governor and three judges but two years later, by an Act of Congress, the Secretary—in case of death, removal, resignation, or necessary absence of the governor—became the acting governor. With such a vast territory to govern it is understandable the governor could be expected to absent himself from the territorial seat of government for lengthy periods as proved the case in future years. Thus, the office of Secretary was an extremely important appointee position.

With a quorum of officials present and necessary to transact business, Governor St. Clair—past president of the Congress and intimately familiar with administrative and legal procedures— began work immediately in typical untiring fashion preparing laws for the pioneer society. He was opposed to rapid introduction of liberal measures in the early government of the territory. One of the first laws enacted by the governor and two judges present provided for a militia in which all men over sixteen years of age were to be enlisted. According to another law, murder and treason were punishable by death; flogging was prescribed for theft; and a fine of ten dimes was to be imposed for drunkenness—if unable to pay the fine the guilty was to serve an hour in the stocks. Citizens were urged to avoid swearing and "idle, vain, and obscene language."

By both innate character, and schooled by the discipline of General Washington during the Revolutionary War, St. Clair had a strong dislike for profane language. He well remembered a General Order written by George Washington in July of 1776 which admonished:

"The General is sorry to be informed that the foolish and wicked practice of profane and cursing and swearing, a vice heretofore little known in an American army, is growing in fashion. He hopes the officers will, by example as well as influence, endeavor to check it, and that both they and the men will reflect, that we can have little hope of the blessing of Heaven on our arms, if we insult it by our impiety and folly. Added to this, it is a vice so mean and low, without any temptation, that every man of sense and character detests and despises it!"

Because of an interpretation of the words of the Ordinance of 1787, the laws of the territory formulated in the early part of St. Clair's administration failed to pass both bodies of Congress and thus the legal structure the governor and judges labored to establish, and set forth in "Laws of the Governor and Judges," were declared null and void. It was not until their meetings of May 29 through August 25, 1795—and while General Anthony Wayne was concluding the Treaty of Greene Ville which opened the Northwest Territory to peaceful settlement—that Governor St. Clair, Judge John Cleves Symmes, and Judge George Turner were able to put together a set of laws which were adopted and published by William Maxwell in Cincinnati (Ohio) as the "Maxwell Code."

In addition to laws governing human behavior, St. Clair and the judges formulated legislation regarding boundaries of the Northwest Territory and on July 27, 1788 Washington County was established—it included almost half the present state of Ohio.

In addition to the large land interests of both the Ohio Company of Associates and the Scioto Company, in the spring of 1787 Benjamin Stites journeyed from southwestern Pennsylvania to New Jersey to tell John Cleves Symmes about the potential of a country he had seen between the Little Miami and Big Miami rivers to the north of the Ohio River. Born in 1742, John Symmes was the eldest son of Reverend Timothy Symmes and Mary, daughter of Captain John Cleves of Long Island. Following a hurried summer visit to this highly touted region, and accompanied by several interested associates, on August 29, 1787 Symmes submitted a petition to Congress to purchase a tract of one million acres between the two Miami rivers under similar terms as that having been submitted by the Ohio Company of Associates. Just as Manasseh Cutler had proposed, Symmes intended to buy the land with government certificates of debt.

But, unable to pay for the entire 600,000 acre tract described in Symme's amended petition of October 2, 1787, his patent issued in 1794 was for only 311,682 acres with the "Miami Purchase" extending north from the Ohio River to the third range of townships. By the contract eventually concluded with the government, Symmes purchased 36,000 acres for himself with 306 warrants and his associate, Jonathan Dayton, used 721 warrants to buy 90,000 acres. The final settlement came only after years of bitter frustrating argument and negotiation with St. Clair and the United States government.

After several abortive thrusts, and a second petition in October of 1787 clarifying his original request for a land grant, John Symmes received what he perceived was a "green light" and the first landing at Columbia in what became known as the "Miami Purchase" was made by Benjamin Stites and his party in late November of 1788. This landing was soon followed in late December of the same year by Messrs Matthias Denman, Robert Patterson, and Israel Ludlow and their party at Yeatman's Cove where Cincinnati, Ohio now stands. Denman had purchased the land opposite the mouth of the Licking River earlier that same year and later sold, for twenty pounds Virginia money, two-thirds of his interest to his partners in this land venture. One of the original partners, John Filson, disappeared during an exploration visit to the area at the mouth of the Great Miami River only a few months earlier and Israel Ludlow picked up his interest. It was John Filson who is credited with originating the name "Losantiville" which the trio called their settlement the first year.

John Armstrong had been offered the appointment as one of the first three judges of the Northwest Territory but he declined and John Cleves Symmes was tendered the appointment at a salary of eight hundred dollars per year. In the summer of 1788 Symmes set out from New Jersey for the western country with a retinue of fourteen four-horse wagons and sixty persons including three carpenters and one mason. It was to be a trying journey and more than six months would elapse before he reached his planned settlement near the mouth of the Great Miami River.

At Bedford, Pennsylvania on August 6, 1788 the judge met Manasseh Cutler at a place where the Symmes party had taken lodging with "a Dutchman" named Mr. West. Cutler was on his way to Marietta and carried a letter for Symmes from his brother Timothy Symmes of Sussex Court House, New Jersey. According to Cutler the Symmes party included one or two women with husbands and "Symmes' daughter Anna was along." Cutler also indicated the entourage Symmes was leading included six heavy wagons, one stage wagon, thirty-one horses, and a "chair" which was a two wheeled covered conveyance for two people. Symmes had been on the road three weeks since leaving New Jersey.

Later that year, as a frustrated John Cleves Symmes pondered his costly delay at Maysville (Kentucky) in late 1788, on December 15th Judge Samuel H. Parsons wrote a letter to Manasseh Cutler who was now back on the east coast. Parsons reported:

"We have had an addition of about one hundred within two weeks. Between forty and fifty houses are so far done as to receive families."

Judge Parsons' report of "about one hundred" may have reflected optimism or some of the former arrivals may have continued on down-stream since various accounts indicate the total population of Marietta at the end of 1788 was between one hundred thirty-two and thirty-seven. James Backus said the settlement's stock consisted of "fifty horses, sixty cows, and seven yoke of oxen."

When John Symmes and his party put in to shore at a point where North Bend (Ohio) would later stand, he did not have the advantage of an adjacent military fortification such as Fort Harmar. Shortly after his arrival two curious Indians of the Shawnee sept, Captain Blackbird and Captain Fig, came to visit him in early February of 1789. Blackbird was fascinated by Symmes' explanation of the seal of the United States—it was the "great eagle" that particularly intrigued him. The lofty flight and great power of this denizen of the sky was well known to the red man.

During the first several years after his arrival at North Bend, Symmes repeatedly urged Governor St. Clair to provide his settlers of the "Miami Purchase" with military protection. In a letter to his business associate back east Symmes bemoaned his plight to General Jonathan Dayton saying:

"Is it a matter of no moment to the United States whether we are saved or destroyed by the savages?"

In January of 1789 St. Clair hosted a conference at Fort Harmar of Indian sachems in an effort to further insure the treaties signed by the red man were agreeable and understood by all. Unfortunately all villages were not represented, particularly those in the western sector of the Northwest Territory.

The first few months of 1789 were busy times in all of the new river settlements. At Marietta the first "town meeting was held on February 4th with Colonel Archibald Crary selected to preside—Ebenezer Battelle was elected clerk. Colonel Ebenezer Sproat had been appointed as Sheriff at Marietta in September of 1788 and now a police board was appointed consisting of Rufus Putnam, Robert Oliver, Griffin Greene, and Nathaniel Goodale.

Fortified by their faith in St. Clair's recently concluded Treaty of Fort Harmar the industrious Marietta immigrants ventured into the surrounding areas and in the spring of 1789 forty settlers established Belpre which extended about five miles along the river 12 miles below the mouth of the Muskinghum. Belpre included Stone's Fort, Newbury, and Farmer's Castle with the latter having 13 cabins. That same spring 39 settlers moved about 25 miles up the Muskinghum to establish themselves at Plainfield (later Waterford) and Fort Frye was built as a refuge. About a half mile away a flour mill was started on Wolf Creek by Major Haffield White, Colonel Robert Oliver, and Captain John Dodge.

These isolated settlements were, unfortunately, easy prey for the Indians who had not accepted "the white man's treaty." Shortly after Reverend Daniel Story arrived at Marietta in the spring of 1789 and held services in the upper story of the northwest blockhouse of Campus Martius, on the first day of May Captain Zebulon King was murdered and scalped at Belpre. The following August two boys were killed just two miles up the Little Kanawha River in Virginia opposite Belpre. A growing alarm began to permeate the thoughts and actions of the settlers.

Undaunted by these hostile acts, the settlers at Belpre opened a school that summer. Notwithstanding the fact there had been a mission school at Schoenbrunn in 1773 and Benjamin Tupper had conducted school in the northwest blockhouse of Campus Martius during the winter of 1788, the school opened at Belpre in 1789 was the first in the Northwest Territory after the Ordinance of 1787.

Motivated by the interest and enthusiasm of Rufus Putnam—and using books he had brought along which had belonged to his birth father, General Israel Putnam—this enterprising pioneer and the settlers of the Belpre area formed the first American circulating library in the Northwest Territory and sold shares for ten dollars each. Captain Sadler, Putnam's stepfather, had been an illiterate according to statements attributed to the superintendent of the Ohio Company of Associates who admonished his descendants:

"Oh, my children, beware you neglect not the education of any under your charge as mine was neglected!"

Aiding and encouraging those about him to live lives of usefulness and labor, historians agree Rufus Putnam was truly one of the foremost builders of Ohio and shared all the hardships of pioneer life with the early settlers of the Territory Northwest of the River Ohio. His profound interest in education was manifest in the Ordinance of 1787. A Federalist, as was Arthur St. Clair, Rufus Putnam was removed from the office of United States Surveyor General in 1803 by President Thomas Jefferson. Rufus Putnam died May 24, 1824 and was laid to rest in Northwest Territory soil.

CHAPTER 12

Banks of the Wabash

"Oh God. He is worse than a murderer! The blood of the slain is upon him—the curse of widows and orphans—the curse of heaven!"

President George Washington
December 19, 1791

Shortly after Isaac Meeks arrived at Marietta in early winter of 1789 and reported there were 72 families and 236 men in the colony, in early January of 1790 Governor Arthur St. Clair moved his territorial headquarters downstream to Losantiville. Upon arriving, and speaking as handsomely as he dressed and looked, St. Clair renamed the settlement "Cincinnati."

The original name had been suggested by John Filson to his real estate partners Matthias Denman and Colonel Patterson. When Filson disappeared in the wilderness country north of the Ohio River and was never heard from again, Israel Ludlow took his place in the three man partnership undertaking of the six hundred forty acre tract of land opposite the mouth of the Licking River. St. Clair selected the new name for the settlement in honor of the Society of The Cincinnati and the strong fortification built to the east of the settlement was named "Fort Washington." Today a monument at Third between Ludlow and Broadway Streets in Cincinnati marks the location of the fort.

Hamilton County was created in January of 1790 before St. Clair continued on downstream to visit Kaskaskia along the

Mississippi—the hazardous 3,000 mile sojourn took almost six months and very nearly cost the 56 year old governor his life when his boat capsized in the icy waters of the Mississippi River. The red-skinned inhabitants of the western region of the Northwest Territory had declined his invitation to peace-talks at Fort Harmar in 1789 so St. Clair decided to visit them and solicit their cooperation in halting the Indian attacks on settlers south of the Ohio River which had provoked increasing concern. St. Clair was particularly concerned the Indians of this far west region sanction the terms of the Treaty of Fort McIntosh as other red sachems had done at Fort Harmar in January of 1789.

During St. Clair's absence the Indians continued their troublesome raids and the pioneer settlers of the area just south of the Ohio River reacted as might be expected with reprisal attacks. Back upstream at Marietta Colonel Ebenezer Sproat commanded 60 militia in building additional fortifications and erected a row of palisades, a line of pickets, and formed a barrier of trees with sharpened boughs as a first line of defense in front of the walls of Campus Martius. The roofs of the stockade buildings were covered with four inches of clay to protect against the Indian's flaming arrows and six scouts made a circuit each morning watching for approaching Indians. During the ensuing Indian trepidations 38 of these scouts were killed in the vicinity of Marietta.

St. Clair returned to Fort Washington in mid-summer of 1790 to find the territory settlers, Judge John Cleves Symmes conspicuous among them, clamoring for military protection against the troublesome Indians. Pausing only briefly for a pensive examination of his family coat of arms, which hung on the wall of his office, the exhausted St. Clair plunged into the many problems awaiting his attention. The inscription on the wall plaque read:

"Commit your work to God."

The inscription was inspirational but the problems which confronted St. Clair were monumental. In an effort to subdue the vexatious red man, and at the suggestion and urging of the Secretary of War, General Josiah Harmar led an expedition north from Fort

73

Washington in October of 1790 intended to demonstrate the nation's power with one sudden decisive blow against the Indian villages. What was planned as a punitive action against the Indians proved unsuccessful and the destruction of the red man's crops and villages only served to further infuriate them. Failing in this attempt to force the Indians to sue for peace, General Harmar led his army back to Fort Washington and subsequently resigned his commission. Flushed with victory, the Indians became even more troublesome and the settlers viewed with ever increasing alarm their precarious position.

As St. Clair, and the top officials of the young government of the United States, pondered their options, on Sunday, January 2, 1791, 30 Wyandots and Delawares attack the Big Bottom settlement north of Marietta—12 settlers were murdered in the assault and five taken captives. Only two men, Asa and Eleazar Bullard, escaped the massacre. The desperate situation the Marietta settlers found themselves faced with was reflected in a letter written January 8, 1791 by Rufus Putnam and addressed to President Washington:

"We have twenty men at Fort Harmar and our civil and military officers do not exceed two hundred eighty-seven badly armed. We are in the utmost danger of being swallowed up, should the enemy push the war with vigor during the winter."

Summoned to Philadelphia for urgent conference, Governor St. Clair was made commander-in-chief of the army and given his former rank of Major General when he proposed to march to Little Turtle's village at the head of the Maumee River establishing intermediate fortifications along the path of march. General Richard Butler was named as St. Clair's second in command and dispatched to recruit men for the expedition.

Leading an undisciplined horde of untrained and ill-equipped raw recruits, and plagued with recurrent attacks of the debilitating gout which is occasioned by exposure, irregular eating habits, and burdensome pressures of overwork, St. Clair led his expedition through the virgin wilderness north from Fort Washington in the fall

74

of 1791. After time-consuming halts to erect Fort Hamilton and Fort Jefferson, St. Clair's expeditionary force reached the banks of the Wabash River where Fort Recovery, Ohio now stands. It was late in the afternoon on November 3, 1791 when the army practically stopped in its tracks forgoing any precaution of building a bulwark against a possible Indian attack.

In addition to non-receipt of sorely needed supplies and the anticipated army payroll which had been promised by government officials as forthcoming but did not actually arrive until January of 1792, the back-breaking march of more than fifty days had taken its toll—morale was low and a loss of men through expiration of six month terms of enlistment had reduced the roll of "effectives" to approximately 1,400. On the night of October 30, 1791 sixty of the Kentucky militia had just "gone home" from the encampment near a huge bog where Camp Sulphur Springs would later stand north of Fort Greene Ville. The next morning St. Clair considered it prudent to dispatch three hundred of the First Regiment of Regulars under Major John Hamtramck in pursuit of the "deserters" in an effort to insure protection for the anticipated supplies reported on the way up the wilderness trail from Fort Washington.

Coupled with all his logistics and morale problems, on the evening of November 3rd of 1791 St. Clair was not aware of his actual position—he thought he was on the banks of the St. Marys River twenty-two miles farther north and within striking distance of Little Turtle's village. He was wrong—almost dead wrong!

Led by Little Turtle and Blue Jacket, the infuriated Indians attack the encampment along the banks of the Wabash at dawn on November 4, 1791 and almost wiped out the expedition—the mortal remains of more than nine hundred brave souls were mercifully covered by a blanket of snow that night as the victorious Indians carried their slain and wounded and ill-gotten loot back towards the Miami village where Fort Wayne, Indiana now stands. The remnants of St. Clair's expedition fled wildly back along the newly blazed wilderness trail toward Fort Jefferson—St. Clair himself was one of the fortunate survivors.

On December 19, 1791 Major Denney delivered to President Washington Arthur St. Clair's battle report. The President's initial reaction was one of anger and reproach but being a fair and just man Washington followed his outburst of rage saying:

"I looked hastily through the dispatches—saw the whole disaster but not all the particulars. St. Clair shall have his justice."

The defeat of St. Clair's army, the single worst carnage in the nation's frontier war history, prompted the first congressional investigation in this country's history. The disastrous defeat also prompted a storm of bitter reproach and abuse which all but broke the spirit and soured the temper of the prostrated governor. Despite his vindication by the investigating committee, the loss of confidence in him by the public was a primary cause of the many difficulties which clouded the closing years of his life of dedicated service. Summarily removed from office as governor in 1802, St. Clair in 1810 was forced to sell his home and property—valued at fifty thousand dollars—for a paltry sum to pay a debt he contracted in 1791 to feed his hungry army. It was a debt the government unjustly refused to honor until it became outlawed.

The task of establishing peace in the Northwest Territory was then given to Anthony Wayne by the President and a worried congress on April 13, 1792 with his appointment as Major General. The wise but aging Little Turtle of the Miamis now cautioned his warriors of this Scotch-Irish officer whom he called "General All-Eyes" saying:

"We have beaten the enemy twice under separate commanders. We cannot expect the same good fortune always. The Americans are now led by a chief who never sleeps. There is something whispers to me that it would be prudent to listen to his offers of peace."

CHAPTER 13

Extirpation

"We have met the enemy and they are ours!"

The situation in the Ohio country had become of serious national consequence following St. Clair's disastrous campaign. Two crushing defeats administered in quick succession prompted even peaceable and inoffensive Indians to now join the war-like warriors and all white settlements were in danger. Despite the provisions of the Treaty of Paris, the British had not evacuated fortifications to the north and were indeed aiding and abetting the inflamed red man's hate for the white encroachers.

With the Indian's successes of 1790 and 1791, the 25 year old Tecumseh of the Shawnees dreamed of a confederation which would enable them to drive the white man back beyond the Allegheny Mountains and openly scoffed at the provisions of the treaties of Fort McIntosh and Fort Harmar which various Indian sachems had signed.

Meantime, prudent as well as bold and self-confident, General Wayne—referred to secretly as "Dandy" by some because of his disciplined manner of dress—carefully planned his campaign taking care to train and discipline his troops of the United States "Legion" as he now called his command. Arriving at Cincinnati in the spring of 1793, "Mad Anthony" Wayne avoided the relative safety of Fort Washington choosing instead to establish "Camp Hobson's Choice" a mile farther downstream where he remained four months providing his troops field training. Captain William Wells—formerly

"Apekonit" of the Miamis and son-in-law of Little Turtle—and Robert McClellan, now joined Anthony Wayne as spies for his army. Wells had been at Little Turtle's side on the banks of the Wabash in early November of 1791 but now this white-man-turned-Indian had again reversed his allegiance.

Marching north from Cincinnati in October of 1793 past Fort Hamilton and proceeding a short distance north of Fort Jefferson, Wayne built a fort which he named in honor of his deceased friend General Nathaniel Greene (1742-1786). Greene had been a leader in the Revolutionary War who some called "the man who saved the south." From Fort Greene Ville in late December of 1793 Wayne dispatched a detachment to the snow covered banks of the Wabash where a fort was built on the site of St. Clair's defeat after first burying many of the mortal remains of those brave souls who had perished there two years before. Wayne had contemplated naming this wilderness outpost "Fort Restitution" but, in placing Captain Alexander Gibson in charge of the garrison of one company of artillery and one of riflemen, he selected "Fort Recovery" as a more suitable name for this stockade.

Throughout the many years since the dreadful carnage of 1791, the residents of the "recovered site" of St. Clair's defeat— several of whom can trace their "roots" to a survivor of the ill-fated expedition—have always remembered the honored dead of this pivotal point in history of the Northwest Territory. In September of 1851 the thoughtful citizens of Fort Recovery joined with hundreds of solemn visitors in a "Bone Burying Day" ceremony wherein the uncovered mortal remains of many who lost their lives along the Wabash were interred. Those same mortal remains were reinterred July 1, 1913 beneath a lofty gray granite shaft which towers above the little village today. Years ago an unknown poet provided posterity with this fitting tribute:

"Then remember their valor, keep holy the sod—
For honor to heroes is glory to God!"

On June 30, 1794 the largest force of Indians ever brought together against a white man's frontier outpost staged a two day assault against Fort Recovery but failed to bring the determined stockade to its knees. The small but impregnable fort repulsed the vicious attack and some historians say it was this battle which broke the back of the Indian's resistance to the white man's advance in the Northwest Territory. Shortly after this unsuccessful attack "The Big Wind," as the Potawatomies now called Wayne, caught up with the Indians downstream from the confluence of the Auglaize and Maumee rivers where he had erected Fort Defiance splitting the enemy's force in half. At the Battle of Fallen Timbers on August 20, 1794 Wayne's army of 2,000 federal and 1,500 militia troops soundly defeated the Indians who now found the doors of the British fort closed when they attempted to retreat to its sanctuary. It was, for all practical purposes, the end of most Indian's hope of pushing the "white invader" back beyond the Allegheny Mountains and talk of peace was being heard around many of the Indian campfires as 1794 came to an end.

Now it was General Wayne, or "Kitcha Shemagana" as some of the Shawnees called him, who called for negotiations. Wayne was an able leader and dedicated to purpose when circumstances demanded it. A loyal admirer of General Washington, in mid-July of 1779—just before the Battle of Stony Point along the Hudson River—Anthony Wayne said to his Revolutionary War commander:

"General Washington sir! If you will only plan it, I will storm hell!"

With equal energy and dedication to the task at hand, in the summer of 1795 Wayne's strong presence was felt around the many "council fires" at Fort Greene Ville as he demanded the treaties of Fort McIntosh and Fort Harmar be ratified. As representative of the United States he asked for additional concessions and grants whereby the Indians ceded 25,000 square miles of land in southeastern Ohio and many other tracts of land in the western part of the region which was to become the state of Ohio. The treaty signed at Fort Greene Ville on August 5, 1795 extended the white man's domain beyond the boundary lines of the Fort McIntosh Treaty of ten years before with the Indians to receive $20,000 in presents and an annuity of $9,500 to be distributed among the signatories. By a later treaty in 1805 the Indians ceded the remainder of the northern part of Ohio to the United States.

With a great respect for General Wayne, Tarhe The Crane—tribal chief of the Wyandots—was very cooperative during the summer negotiations of 1795 at Fort Greene Ville and was given a copy of the treaty for safe keeping among the Indians. The document consisted of two sheets of parchment as big as a door and was signed by eighty Indians along with General Wayne and his staff. This was to be Anthony Wayne's final great achievement and, suffering from ill health brought on by repeated exposure, he died at Erie, Pennsylvania December 15, 1796.

With the Treaty of Greene Ville signed it was the Virginians who swarmed the Military Tract reserved in her cession for bounty lands. The immigration was led by Colonel Nathaniel Massie who settled Manchester on the Ohio River and later—together with Duncan McArthur—laid out Chillicothe in 1796. In 1795 Connecticut sold the remainder of its Western Reserve and Moses Cleaveland established the city of Cleveland the following year. Franklintown (now Columbus, Ohio) was laid out in 1797 as the population of the Northwest Territory continued to grow.

Surveyed by an Act of Congress June 1, 1796 the United States Military Lands covered an area from the northwest corner of the Seven Ranges south fifty miles, west to the Scioto River, north along the river to the Greene Ville Treaty Line, and then east. The area was divided into five mile square townships and owners of the land tracts therein received patents signed by the President of the United States. In 1798 Congress passed legislation ratifying an April of 1783 promise to refugees who abandoned British provinces in Canada and Nova Scotia and on February 18, 1801 an act set apart fractional townships of the 16th through 22nd ranges of townships joining the southern border of the Military Lands. The tract was about four and one half miles wide extending 42 miles east of the Scioto River—Columbus, Ohio founded in 1812 partially lies in this "Refugee Tract."

To be of immediate service to those interested in purchasing land in the territory that was to become Ohio, Congress established land offices at Marietta, Cincinnati, Steubenville, Chillicothe, Zanesville, Canton, Wooster, Piqua, Delaware, Wapakoneta, Lima, and Upper Sandusky. In these offices information was available regarding land in the Seven Ranges, French Grant, and Refugee's Tract.

The rapid influx of settlers enabled the Northwest Territory to achieve the second state of government provided for in the Ordinance of 1787 and by authorization of September 16, 1799 the first elected legislature met on September 24th in Cincinnati with twenty-two in the House of Representatives and five in the Senate (or Council). William Henry Harrison was chosen the first territorial delegate to Congress. The new legislature tried to take its business out of the hands of the governor but, as provided for in the Ordinance of 1787, such action was promptly overruled by Governor St. Clair's veto. Meantime, Edward Tiffin, Nathaniel Massie, Thomas Worthington, and Jeremiah Morrow pushed forward the organization of a state government.

As provided for in the opening paragraph of the all important Ordinance of 1787, by an Act of Congress May 7, 1800 the Northwest Territory was divided into two districts as follows:

"That from and after the 4th of July next, all that part of the territory of the United States northwest of the Ohio River which lies to the westward of a line beginning at the Ohio, opposite to the mouth of the Kentucky River, and thence north until it shall intersect the territorial line between the United States and Canada, shall for the purpose of temporary government, constitute a separate territory, and be called the Indiana Territory."

The territorial delegate to Congress, William Henry Harrison, was appointed governor of the Indiana Territory which had a population approximating 5,641 with about 1,500 people living around Vincennes and the rest on the Clark grant (Clarksville, Indiana). Corydon succeeded Vincennes as the territorial capital in 1813 and Indiana was admitted to the Union December 11, 1816 by an Act of Congress approved April 19, 1816. The capital was established at Indianapolis in 1825.

The country east of the Indian Territory boundary line was still to be called the Northwest Territory with its seat at Chillicothe. The line between the mouth of the Kentucky River and Fort Recovery was one of the boundary lines established by the Treaty of Greene Ville. By census of 1802 the population of the eastern area was reported to be 45,028.

With a liberal interpretation of the provisions of Article V of the Ordinance of 1787, on April 20, 1802 Congress authorized the eastern division to draft a state (Ohio) constitution and obliged them to accept an east-west line drawn through the southerly extreme of Lake Michigan as the northern boundary west of Lake Erie. The arbitrary decision sparked later controversy since a Department of State map in the nation's capital placed the southern bend of Lake Michigan at 42 degrees 20 minutes or about twelve miles north of its actual location. On January 11, 1805 Congress erected the Michigan Territory and there ensued a dispute regarding its southern boundary which was not totally resolved until January 26, 1837 when Michigan was admitted to the Union with its present boundaries.

But it was during 1802, and while 35 delegates were drafting an Ohio constitution at Chillicothe, when Governor St. Clair—an ardent Federalist who stood by George Washington and had supported President John Adams—became involved with the political doctrine of the newly elected President Thomas Jefferson. At Chillicothe in early November of 1802 St. Clair made an impassioned speech which prompted his dismissal as governor November 22nd and Charles William Byrd was named as his successor.

The staunch old Federalist and self-sacrificing patriot retired to his home near Ligonier in Pennsylvania where in a few years he was forced to sell his property to liquidate an indebtedness incurred while trying to feed and clothe his army during the disastrous expedition of 1791. St. Clair died in abject poverty August 31, 1818 at 84 years of age when a wagon upset leaving the old veteran alone and insensible on the ground. Having given so much of his personal life and wealth to his adopted country, one 19th century historian declared he should

82

have been classed with superior men of foreign birth such as Baron Von Steuben, the Marquis de Lafayette, and Russian born Alexander Procofieff De Seversky. It is unfortunate St. Clair's defeat on the banks of the Wabash over-shadowed his many accomplishments and years of dedicated service to the nation.

Congress passed an enabling act November 29, 1802 under which the Ohio constitution was completed at Chillicothe where action on it had started November 1st. The constitution was adopted without referring it to the people—it remained unaltered for fifty years. An election was held on January 11, 1803 in which English born Edward Tiffin (1766-1829) was elected the first governor of Ohio and the first legislature of the state of Ohio met in Chillicothe on March 1, 1803.

Ohio was admitted to the Union as the seventeenth state—the first state to be carved out of the Northwest Territory. The state legislature held sessions in Chillicothe until 1810 when a law was passed fixing the seat of state government at Zanesville. Here the lawmakers met until 1812, at which time it was decided to make Columbus the permanent seat of state government. The capital was again moved to Chillicothe until suitable buildings could be erected in Columbus—this was completed in 1816.

General William Hull was named governor of the Michigan Territory in 1805 a little more than a century after French explorer Antoine de la Mothe Cadillac established Fort Pont Chartrain in 1701 at the place where Detroit would later stand. Michigan achieved statehood in 1837. Wisconsin formed her state constitution August 6, 1846 and was admitted to the Union May 29, 1848. Technically, the Ordinance of 1787 provided for only five states but that portion of the Minnesota Territory east of the Mississippi River was an "adjustment" made by Congress. A land boom started in 1848 at St. Paul and the region grew quickly—Minnesota with its present boundaries was admitted to the Union May 11, 1858. Thus, seventy-one years after adoption of the Ordinance of Freedom, territorial acquisition and division among its six states was complete.

Problems with the Indians of the Northwest Territory were quieted early in the 19th century. Although Catahecassa (Black Hoof) and the white-man-turned-Indian, Blue Jacket, participated,

Tecumseh of the same Shawnee sept refused to either attend the negotiations or sign the Treaty of Greene Ville. After 1795 Tecumseh made trips to the Indian villages along the northern Mississippi River and circulated through the states of Kentucky and Georgia and areas later known as Alabama and Tennessee. Everywhere he visited Tecumseh told of his dream of a union of red men similar to the white man's "council of thirteen fires." His dream of an Indian confederation might have been successful had it not been for the Battle of Tippecanoe November 7, 1811 which served to weaken the smoldering red man's resistance and Tecumseh never again regained his growing position of leadership.

At least one historian credits Tecumseh's brother, Tenskawatawa—or Prophet—as being the primary force in the Indian movement during the first decade of the 1800s. Prophet certainly acquired a strong hold on the superstitious mind of his followers and added fuel to the fire of the Indian's hatred of the "white invaders." The idea of a political confederation as advocated by Tecumseh and his brother was the last desperate attempt by the Indians to hold a line against the white man's continued encroachment and had the unification endeavor been successful—or had General Wayne's 1794 campaign been unsuccessful—the history of the Northwest Territory would have been written differently.

In 1812 a serious blow was given the interests of the United States when Governor William Hull of the Michigan Territory surrendered Detroit to British General Sir Isaac Brock and his Indian allies. William Hull (1753-1825) had been an officer in the Revolutionary War and his fine military record was all that saved him from being shot in 1814 after being court-martialed and found guilty of cowardice and neglect of duty in action against the British along the banks of the "Dardanelles of America" where Detroit stood. By this single stroke all of Michigan and much of Indiana and Illinois fell into the hands of the British and Indians—the Indians massacred many of the white settlers at Fort Dearborn (Chicago) in the ensuing period.

President James Madison, sometimes called the "Father of the United States Constitution" because he planned the system of checks and balances between the legislative, executive, and judicial branches of the government, had known for some time war with Great Britain was a distinct possibility. Madison knew the young nation was not prepared for war but could not ignore the public clamors for action against Great Britain and finally was forced to recommend to Congress a declaration of war. On June 18, 1812 by a House vote of 79 to 49 and a Senate vote of 19 to 13, Congress approved the declaration of war and General William Henry Harrison was dispatched to the Maumee River area in hope of regaining the initiative.

While twenty-one year old Colonel George Croghan at Fort Stephenson (Lower Sandusky) held his post with a handful of gallant men and a single field gun in early August of 1813 against two thousand British and Indians who staged an unsuccessful two day assault, on nearby Lake Erie a British Squadron of eight vessels were a menace to Ohio—a situation which Commodore Oliver Perry of Rhode Island had been sent to meet. Nine ships were built at Erie, Pennsylvania and in September of 1813 the British and American fleets faced each other at the head of Lake Erie west of Put-in-Bay and much depended upon the outcome. If the British won, Ohio was open to invasion and the entire Northwest Territory would be in jeopardy. If Perry was victorious the Americans were ready to invade Canada. On September 10, 1813 the British "Detroit" lowered her colors and Major General Harrison received the now famous dispatch from Oliver Hazard Perry:

"We have met the enemy and they are ours—two ships, two brigs, one schooner, and one sloop."

Close on the heels of this important Lake Erie triumph was the defeat of retreating British General Proctor and his Indian allies by General Harrison's troops in the Battle of the Thames east of Detroit in Canada. It was this battle which saw the death of Tecumseh and heralded the end of all hope of British victory in the Northwest Territory—the glory of the Indian sun set with the death of Tecumseh. The Treaty of Ghent signed December 24, 1814 at

85

Ghent, Belgium signaled the end of the War of 1812 and it was ratified by the United States February 17, 1815.

William Henry Harrison, leader of the military force of the Northwest Territory during the War of 1812, was nominated by a National Whig Convention for the presidency in December of 1839. He was elected decisively but died April 4, 1841 only 31 days after his inauguration.

In 1818 the northwest part of the state of Ohio was acquired by the United States in a treaty with the Indians subject to certain reservations all of which were subsequently quieted with the lands ceded to the government. A final treaty with the Wyandots was signed in 1842 when the last remnant of seven hundred Indians moved to Kansas—the Indians of the Northwest Territory were no more.

With the end of the Indian danger men began to cultivate their fields in peace and the settlements of the Northwest Territory grew rapidly. In 1801 a one hundred ton vessel was built at Marietta and made its maiden voyage to New Orleans. In 1811 the wood-burning steamboat "New Orleans" was traveling the waters of the Ohio River. The legislature of Ohio authorized the building of two canals—in 1832 the Ohio and Erie canal joined Cleveland and Portsmouth and in 1843 a man-made waterway facilitated travel between Toledo and Cincinnati. In similar ambitious undertakings the entire region of the Northwest Territory took on a glow of activity as the spirit and energy of the early pioneer settler's descendants continued to make the region blossom.

Among the dog-eared pages of a time-worn history of Ohio a poem by E.A. Jones appropriately says:

> "Illustrious men! Though slumbering in the dust
> You still are honored by the Good and just.
> Posterity will shed a conscious tear
> And pointing say, 'There lies a pioneer!'"

The Ordinance of 1787

An Ordinance for the Government of the Territory of the United States Northwest of the River Ohio.

Be it ordained by the United States, in Congress assembled, That the said Territory, for the purposes of temporary government, be one district; subject, however, to be divided into two districts, as future circumstances may, in the opinion of Congress, make it expedient.

Be it ordained by the authority aforesaid, That the estates both of resident and non-resident proprietors in the said Territory, dying intestate, shall descend to and be distributed among their children and the descendants of a deceased child in equal parts; the descendants of a deceased child or grandchild to take the share of their deceased parent in equal parts among them; and where there shall be no children or descendants, then in equal parts to the next of kin, in equal degree; and among collaterals, the children of a deceased brother or sister of the intestate shall have in equal parts among them their deceased parent's share; and there shall in no case be a distinction between kindred of the whole and the half-blood; saving in all cases to the widow of the intestate her third part of the real estate for life, and one-third part of the personal estate; and this law relative to descents and dower shall remain in full force until altered by the legislature of the district. And until the governor and judges shall adopt laws as hereinafter mentioned, estates in the said Territory may be devised or bequeathed by wills in writing signed and sealed by him or her in whom the estate may (being of full age) and attested by three witnesses; and real estates may be conveyed by lease and release, or bargain and sale, signed, sealed, and delivered by the person, being of full age, in whom the estate may be, and attested by two witnesses, provided such wills be duly proved, and such conveyances be acknowledged, or the execution thereof duly proved, and be recorded within one year after a proper magistrate, courts, and registers, shall be appointed for that purpose; and personal property may be transferred by delivery, saving, however, to the French and Canadian inhabitants, and other settlers of the Kaskaskias, St. Vincennes, and the neighboring villages, who have heretofore professed themselves citizens of Virginia, their laws and customs now in force among them relative to the descent and conveyance of property.

Be it ordained by the authority aforesaid, That there shall be appointed, from time to time, by Congress, a governor, whose commission shall continue in force for the term of three years, unless sooner revoked by Congress: he shall reside in the district and have a freehold estate therein, in one thousand acres of land, while in the exercise of his office.

There shall be appointed, from time to time, by Congress, a secretary, whose commission shall continue in force for four years, unless sooner revoked; he shall reside in the district, and have a freehold estate therein, in five hundred acres of land, while in the exercise of his office. It shall be his duty to keep and preserve the acts and laws passed by the legislature, and the public records of the district and the proceedings of the governor in his executive department, and transmit authentic copies of such acts and proceedings every six months to the Secretary of Congress.

There shall also be appointed a court, to consist of three judges, any two of whom to form a court, who shall have a common-law jurisdiction, and reside in the district, and have each therein a freehold estate, in five hundred acres of land, while in the exercise of their offices; and their commission shall continue in force during good behavior.

The governor and judges, or a majority of them, shall adopt and publish in the district such laws of the original States, criminal and civil, as may be necessary and best suited to the circumstances of the district, and report them to Congress from time to time, which laws shall be in force in the district until the organization of the General Assembly therein, unless disapproved by the Congress; but afterwards the legislature shall have the authority to alter them as they shall think fit. The governor for the time being, shall be commander-in-chief of the militia, and appoint and commission all officers in the same below the rank of general officers; all general officers shall be appointed and commissioned by Congress.

Previous to the organization of the General Assembly, the governor shall appoint such magistrates and other civil officers in each county or township as he shall find necessary for the preservation of the peace and good order in the same. After the General Assembly shall be organized, the powers and duties of magistrates and other civil officers shall be regulated and defined by the said Assembly; but all magistrates and other civil officers, not herein otherwise directed, shall, during the continuance of this temporary government, be appointed by the governor.

For the prevention of crimes and injuries, the laws to be adopted or made shall have force in all parts of the district, and for the execution of process, criminal and civil, the governor shall make proper divisions thereof; and he shall proceed, from time to time, as circumstances may require, to layout the parts of the district in which the Indian title shall have been extinguished, into counties and townships, subject, however, to such alterations as may thereafter be made by the legislature.

So soon as there shall be five thousand free male inhabitants, of full age, in the district, upon giving proof therefore to the governor, they shall receive authority, with time and place, to elect representatives from their counties or townships, to represent them in the General Assembly: provided, that, for every five hundred free male inhabitants, there shall be one representative, and so on progressively with the number of free male inhabitants shall the right of representation increase, until the number of representatives shall amount to twenty-five; after which the number and proportion of representatives shall be regulated by the legislature: provided, that no person shall be eligible or qualified to act as a representative, unless he shall have been a citizen of one of the United States three years, and be a resident in the district, or unless he shall have resided in the district three years, and, in either case, he shall likewise hold in his own right, in fee simple, two hundred acres of land within the same: provided, also, that a freehold in fifty acres of land in the district, having been a citizen of one of the States, and being resident in the district, or the like freehold and two year's residence in the district, shall be necessary to qualify a man as an elector of a representative.

The representatives thus elected shall serve for the term of two years; and, in case of the death of the representative, or removal from office, the governor shall issue a writ to the county or township for which he was a member, to elect another in his stead, to serve for the residue of the term.

The General Assembly, or legislature, shall consist of a governor, legislative council, and a House of Representatives. The legislative council shall consist of five members to continue in office five years, unless sooner removed by Congress, any three of whom to be a quorum, and the members of the council shall be nominated and appointed in the following manner, to-wit: As soon as representatives shall be elected, the governor shall appoint a time and place for them to meet together, and, when met, they shall nominate ten persons, residents of the district, and each possessed of a freehold in five hundred acres of land, and return their names to Congress; five of whom Congress shall appoint and commission to serve as aforesaid; and whenever a vacancy shall happen in the council, by death or removal from office, the House of Representatives shall nominate two persons, qualified as aforesaid, for each vacancy, and return their names to Congress; one of whom Congress shall appoint and commission for the residue of the term; and every five years, four months at least before the expiration of the time of service of the members of the council, the said House shall nominate ten persons, qualified as aforesaid, and return their names to Congress, five of whom Congress shall appoint and commission to serve as members of the council five years unless sooner removed. And the governor, legislative council, and House of Representatives, shall have authority to make laws in all cases, for the good government of the district, not repugnant to the principles and articles in this ordinance established and declared. And all bills having passed by a majority in the House, and by a majority in the council, shall be referred to the governor for his assent; but no bill or legislative act whatever shall be of any force without his assent. The governor shall have power to convene, prorogue, and dissolve the General Assembly, when, in his opinion, it shall be expedient.

The governor, judges, legislative council, secretary, and other such officers as Congress shall appoint in the district, shall take an oath or affirmation of fidelity and of office; the governor before the president of Congress, and all other officers before the governor. As soon as a legislature shall be formed in the district, the council and House, assembled in one room, shall have authority by joint ballot to elect a delegate to Congress, who shall have a seat in Congress, with a right of debating, but not of voting, during this temporary government.

And for extending the fundamental principles of civil and religious liberty, which form the basis whereon these republics, their laws, and constitutions are erected; to fix and establish those principles as the basis of all laws, constitutions, and governments which forever hereafter be formed in the said territory; to provide also for the establishment of States, and permanent government therein, and for their admission to a share in the Federal councils, on an equal footing with the original States, at as early periods as may be consistent with the general interest.

It is hereby ordained and declared by the authority aforesaid, That the following articles shall be considered as articles of compact between the original States and the people and States in the said territory, and forever remain unalterable, unless by common consent, to wit:

ARTICLE I. No person demeaning himself in a peaceable and orderly manner shall ever be molested on account of his mode of worship or religious sentiments in the said territory.

ARTICLE II. The inhabitants of the said territory shall always be entitled to the benefits of the writ of habeas corpus and of trial by jury; of a proportionate representation of the people in the legislature, and of judicial proceedings according to the course of the common law. All persons shall be bailable, unless for capital offenses, where the proof shall be evident or the presumption great; all fines shall be moderate, and no cruel or unusual punishments shall be inflicted: No man shall be deprived of his liberty or property but by the judgment of his peers, or the law of the land; and should the public exigencies make it necessary, for the common preservation, to take any person's property, or to demand his particular services, full compensation shall be made for the same; and, in the just preservation of rights and property, it is understood and declared that no law ought ever to be made, or have force in the said territory, that shall, in any manner whatever, interfere with or affect private contracts or engagements bona fide and without fraud, previously formed.

ARTICLE III. Religion, morality, and knowledge, being necessary to good government and the happiness of mankind, schools and the means of education shall forever be encouraged. The utmost good faith shall always be observed toward the Indians; their lands and property shall never be taken from them without their consent; and, in their property, rights, and liberty, they never shall be invaded or disturbed, unless in just and lawful wars authorized by Congress; but laws founded in justice and humanity shall, from time to time, be made, for preventing wrongs being done to them and for preserving peace and friendship with them.

ARTICLE IV. The said territory and the States which may be formed therein, shall forever remain a party of this Confederacy of the United States of America, subject to the Articles of Confederation and to such alterations therein as shall constitutionally be made; and to all the acts and ordinances of the United States, in Congress assembled, conformable thereto. The inhabitants and settlers in the said territory shall be subject to pay a part of the Federal debts, contracted or to be contracted, and a proportional part of the expenses of government, to be apportioned on them by Congress, according to the same common rule and measure by which apportionments thereof shall be made on the other States; and the taxes for paying their proportion shall be laid and levied by the authority and direction of the legislatures of the district or districts, or new States, as in the original States, within the time agreed upon by the United States, in Congress assembled. The legislatures of those districts, or new States, shall never interfere with the primary disposal of the soil by the United States, in Congress assembled, nor with any regulations Congress may find necessary for securing the title in such soil to the bona fide purchasers. No tax shall be imposed on lands the property of the United States; and in no case shall non-resident proprietors be taxed higher than residents. The navigable water leading into the Mississippi and St. Lawrence, and the carrying- places between the same shall be common highways and forever free, as well to the inhabitants of the said territory as to the citizens of the United States, and those of any other States that may be admitted into the Confederacy, without any tax impost, or duty therefor.

ARTICLE V. There shall be formed in the said territory not less than nor more than five States; and the boundaries of the States, as soon as Virginia shall alter her act of cession and consent to the same, shall become fixed and established as follows to-wit: The western State in the said territory shall be bounded by the Mississippi, the Ohio, and the Wabash Rivers; a direct line drawn from the Wabash and Post Vincent's due north to the territorial line between the United States and Canada, and by the said territorial line to the Lake of the Woods and Mississippi. The middle State shall be bounded by the said direct line, the Wabash from Post Vincent's to the Ohio; by the Ohio, by a direct line drawn due north from the mouth of the Great Miami to the said territorial line and by the said territorial line. The eastern State shall be bounded by the last-mentioned direct line, the Ohio, Pennsylvania, and the said territorial line; provided, however, and it is further understood and declared, that the boundaries of these three States shall be subject so far to be altered, that if Congress shall hereafter find it expedient, they shall have authority to form one or two States in that part of the said territory which lies north of an east and west line drawn through the southerly bend or extreme of Lake Michigan and whenever any of the said States shall have sixty thousand free inhabitants therein, such State shall be admitted by its delegates into the Congress of the United States on an equal footing with the original States, in all respects whatever; and shall be at liberty to form a permanent constitution and State government; provided, the constitution and government so to be formed shall be republican and in conformity to the principles contained in these articles; and, so far as it can be consistent with the general interest of the Confederacy, such admissions shall be allowed at an earlier period, and when there may be a less number of free inhabitants in the States than sixty thousand.

ARTICLE VI. There shall be neither slavery nor involuntary servitude in the said territory, otherwise than in punishment of crimes whereof the party shall have been duly convicted; provided, always, that any person escaping into the same, from whom labor or service is lawfully claimed in any one of the original States, such fugitives may be lawfully reclaimed and conveyed to the person claiming his or her labor or service as aforesaid.

Be it ordained by the authority aforesaid, That the resolutions of the 23rd of April, 1784, relative to the subject of this ordinance, be and the same are hereby repealed and declared null and void.

Done by the United States in Congress assembled, on the 13th day of July, in the year of our Lord 1787, and of their sovereignty and independence the 12th.

Chas. Thomson, Sec'y.

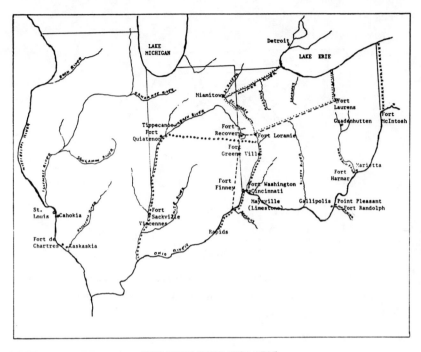

TREATY LINES 1784-1795

xxxx   Fort Stanwix, October 22, 1784—Six nations: Mohawks,
        Oneidas, Senecas, Cayugas, Onondagas, Tuscaroras. Included
        treaty lines in Pennsylvania and New York also.

. . . .   Fort McIntosh, Jan. 21, 1785—Wyandots, Delawares, Ottawas,
        and Chippewas.

oooo   Fort Finney, Jan. 31, 1786—Shawnees, Delawares, Wyandots,
        and Ottawas.

*   Fort Harmar, January, 1789—Six Nations and Wyandots,
        Ottawas, Delawares, Chippewas, Potawatomies, Sacs.

- - - -   Fort Greene Ville, Aug. 5, 1795

        * Confirming Fort McIntosh Treaty Lines

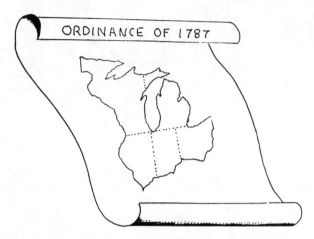

TERRITORY OF THE UNITED STATES NORTHWEST OF THE RIVER OHIO
(with future state boundaries as specified by the Ordinance of 1787)

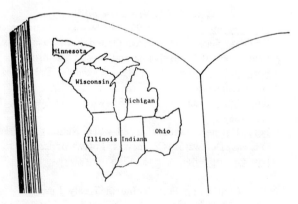

"...that ordinance was constantly looked to whenever a new territory was to become a state. Congress always traced their course by the Ordinance of 1787."

Abraham Lincoln

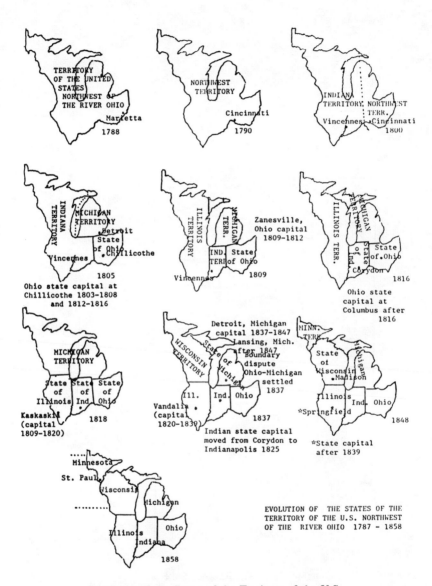

Evolution of the States of the Territory of the U.S.
Northwest of the River Ohio, 1787-1858

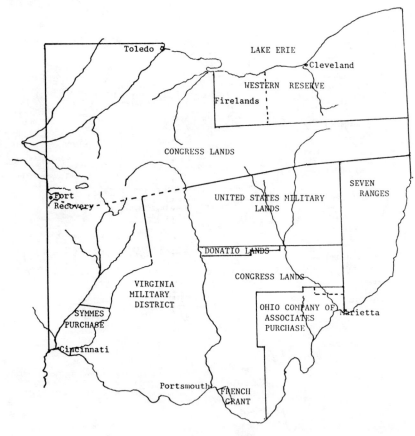

The Buckeye State

BIBLIOGRAPHY

The Draper Manuscripts, by Dr. Lyman Copeland Draper, Wisconsin Historical Society Library, Madison, Wisconsin.

Ohio Laws (1833) by Chief Justice Salmon Portland Chase (1808-1873).

The Ohio Company, by Julia Perkins Cutler (b. 1815).

The Ohio Country by Charles E. Slocum (1783-1815).

Biographical and Historical Memoirs of the Early Pioneer Settlers of Ohio, (1852) by Dr. Samuel Prescott Hildreth (1783-1863).

Life Among the Indians (1857) by James B. Finley.

The Military Journal of Ebenezer Denny , published 1860 by the Pennsylvania Historical Society, J.B. Lippincot & Company.

A History of the War of 1812 in the Northwest, (1872) by William S. Hatch.

History of the Maumee Valley,(1873) by Horace S. Knapp.

Simon Girty, (1873) by Consul W. Butterfield.

Journal of Stephen Ruddell, (1882) by Stephen Ruddell, Greene County Public Library, Xenia, Ohio.

Memoirs of Benjamin Van Cleve, Manuscript, Montgomery County Public Library, Dayton, Ohio.

A History of the United States, A.D. 432 to 1886, (1886) by Robert James Belford Published by The World, New York City.

History of the Girtys, (1890) Robert Clarke & Co., Cincinnati, Ohio.

Historical Collections of Ohio, Vol. I (1847) and Vol. II (1888), by Henry Howe (1816-1893) & Son, Columbus, Ohio

The St. Clair Papers, Life and Public Service of Arthur St. Clair, Vol. 2 (1882) by William Henry Smith.

The Northwest Under Three Flags, 1635-1796, (1900) Charles Moore.

History of the Ordinance of 1787, (9 June 1856) by Edward Coles Pennsylvania Historical Society Publications

History of Michigan, (1839) by J.H. Lanham.

History of Illinois (1844) by Henry Brown.

History of Indiana,(1879) by Logan Esarey

History of Minnesota (1882) by E. D. Neill

The Treaty of Greene Ville,(1894) by Frazer Ells Wilson.

Conquest of the Old Northwest, (1901) by James Baldwin.

History of Scioto County, (1903) by Nelson W. Evans.

Wisconsin in Three Centuries, (1905) by Reuben G. Thwaites.

Early Western Travels, 1746-1846, (1904) Reuben Thwaites, Ed., Cleveland, Ohio.

Tecumseh and the Shawnee Prophet, (1906) Edward Eggleston, et al.

The Peace of Mad Anthony, (1907) by Frazer Ells Wilson.

Arthur St. Clair of Old Fort Recovery, (1911) by S.A.D. Whipple.

Little Turtle, (1917) by Calvin M. Young.

Winning of the West, (1920) by Theodore Roosevelt.

Territorial Papers of the U.S., Northwest Territory, Vol. III (1934), Clarence E. Carter, Washington, D.C.

General Josiah Harmar Papers, William L. Clements Library, University of Michigan, Ann Arbor.

OHIO ARCHEOLOGICAL AND HISTORICAL SOCIETY PUBLICATIONS
Beginning of the Ohio Company (1895), Vol. IV
Tecumseh, by Emilius O. Randall (1906) Vol. XV
Sinclaire's Defeat, Vol. XV
Memoirs of Benjamin Van Cleve, Vol. XVII
Fort Recovery, and *Major George Adams, 1767-1832,* Vol. XXII, (1913) by George A. Katzenberger
Diary of Winthrop Sargent, (1910), Vol. XIX

Historical Sketch of Fort Recovery, (1941) by Martha E. Rohr, Journal Publishing Company, Fort Recovery, Ohio

Fort Recovery, Scene of Bloody Massacre, (1955) by Robert V. Van Trees, *The Journal Gazette,* Sect. E, Ft. Wayne, Indiana, 29 May 1955.